A Treasury of
Texas Tales

A Treasury of
Texas Tales

Webb Garrison

RUTLEDGE HILL PRESS®
Nashville, Tennessee

Published in Nashville, Tennessee, by Rutledge Hill Press®, 211 Seventh Avenue North, Nashville, Tennessee 37219. Distributed in Canada by H. B. Fenn & Company, Ltd., 34 Nixon Road, Bolton, Ontario L7E 1W2.

Typography by E. T. Lowe Typesetting, Inc., Nashville, Tennessee.

Library of Congress Cataloging-in-Publication Data

Garrison, Webb, 1919–
    A treasury of Texas tales / Webb Garrison.
          p.   cm.
    Includes index.
    ISBN 978-1-55853-537-4
    1. Texas—History—Anecdotes.   2. Texas—Biography—
Anecdotes.   I. Title.
    F386.6.G37   1997
    976.4—dc21   97-32308
                                                                          CIP

Printed in the United States of America.

1 2 3 4 5 6 7 8 9—99 98 97

Contents

Preface   7

Part 1: Trailblazers
1. Stephen F. Austin—Land Agent   11
2. Samuel P. Colt—The Texas Revolver   18
3. Babe Didrikson—One-Woman Team   25
4. Gail Borden—Lucky Dabbler   29
5. Waylon Jennings—Platinum Outlaw   35
6. Ann Richards—Out But Not Down   40
7. Texas City—Deadly Prelude   46

Part 2: Off the Beaten Path
8. Lady Bird—Percentage Points   53
9. Galveston—Curse Reversed   58
10. Zachary Taylor—A Second Career   66
11. O. Henry—Spare Time   71

Part 3: Westward Ho!
12. Sam Houston—From Wayward Son to Revolutionary Father   79
13. Joanna Troutman—The Betsy Ross of Texas   85
14. James W. Fannin—Sudden Death at Goliad   90

Part 4: Raw Courage
15. Theodore H. Barrett—The Last Hurrah   97
16. Travis, Bowie, and Crockett—The Alamo   103
17. Barbara Jordan—Captive Listener   110
18. John Magruder—Hot Spot   115
19. Dan Rather—Courage!   122
20. San Jacinto—Sixteen Minutes to Independence   129
21. Valverde, New Mexico—Iron Hail   135

Part 5: A Matter of Timing
22. Robert E. Lee—By the Skin of His Teeth   141
23. Sabine Pass—Victory or Death!   149
24. Mirabeau Buonaparte Lamar—Turn Around   156
25. Quanah Parker—The Last Comanche Chieftain   162
26. Chester W. Nimitz—Old Graduate   169

Part 6: Mavericks, Strays, and Zealots
27. Gen. Antonio López de Santa Anna—
    Serene Highness   177
28. Andrew Jackson—Political Clout   182
29. Ben McCulloch—A Rare Breed   185
30. John R. Brinkley—500,000 Watts   192
31. Jefferson Davis—Ships of the Desert   198
32. Ross Perot—Never Give Up!   202

Bibliography   207
Index   211

Preface

Any brief attempt to describe the Lone Star State is futile. When such an effort is made, language fails. Texas is gigantic, and eight flags have succeeded one another in flying over part or all of it: Spanish, French, Spanish again, Mexican, Republic of Texas, United States, Confederate, and United States for a second time.

The state sprawls across 267,339 square miles—making it nearly 100,000 square miles larger than California and more than fifty times the size of Connecticut. Its southernmost point is separated from its northernmost by almost 800 miles, while its most eastern point is more than 800 miles from its most western point.

Not far from the state's coast, which is short only by comparison with its immense land-locked boundaries, Brownsville is nearly four hundred miles south of Juárez, Mexico. In the Lone Star State, four great geographical regions meet: the Great Plains, the North-Central Plains, the Coastal Plains, and the Trans-Pecos Region.

Among present-day states, only Texas was once an independent republic that plunged the United States into war with a foreign nation. Near Beaumont, the Spindletop oil field ushered the nation and much of the Western world into the petroleum age.

Native Americans, who once occupied most of the vast region, left a permanent verbal legacy when their word for a confederation of tribes, *tejas*, became *Texas* soon after the first Anglos arrived. Spanish-speaking Texans enriched the vocabulary, not only of the future state, but also of the nation of which it became a part.

San Antonio, El Paso, Corpus Christi, and hosts of other cities and towns have Spanish names; so does the Rio Grande and many other physical features of the state. Even the Colorado River gets its name from a modification of the descriptive term meaning "reddish," which it still is in some seasons. Many Spanish words or slightly altered variants of them are commonly used by Americans with no need of translation or explanation. A few of these are rodeo, plaza, canal, patio, vista, hombre, desperado, and amigo.

It doesn't take a linguist to see that *el lagarto* was transformed into *alligator*, or that *huracan* was the parent of *hurricane*. The *lazo* used by early Spanish riders became the cowboy's *lasso*, and *barbecue* was once *el barbacoa*.

It is no wonder that in such a land, colorful and forceful people have always abounded. To Texans, everything in Texas is bigger and everything is better. Since only a handful of the Lone Star State's significant men and women can be treated in a single slim volume such as this, it is hoped that this book will lead you to delve more deeply into the many dimensions of the story of Texas.

Part One
Trailblazers

Stephen F. Austin took over where his father left off, but despite his monumental contributions he never became president of the republic.

1
Stephen F. Austin
Land Agent

The story of Texas begins with the land. Like most tales of the West, the plains were open and there was hardly a person in sight when the Spanish conquistadors first saw the Texas coast in 1528. The lack of civilization also meant that the Spanish were slow to settle the area. The French were no more successful than the Spanish, but by the early nineteenth century many Americans were anxious to occupy the fertile wilderness.

Affluent J. T. Lamar of Georgia owed much of his prosperity to land speculation. Like many other influential men in his state, Lamar skirted the law when Cherokee land was offered in lotteries. Writing to a friend in Alabama in 1836, he pointed to what he considered a new source of sure wealth:

> Let me advise you to come on with all the money you can command & invest in Texas lands—no such speculations were ever offered on this continent, and capitalists who will purchase now will make overwhelming fortunes.
>
> The lands are the richest on the face of the globe, and the titles indisputable. No one can possibly lose who will embark in the speculation—Dont think I exaggerate when I tell you that Texas is capable with proper cultivation to produce as much cotton as is made in all the United States.

Rapid population growth in most regions east of the Mississippi River caused adventurers to move west soon after Thomas Jefferson's great gamble of 1803: the Louisiana Purchase. Within the two decades after Jefferson acted without congressional authorization—pledging to pay France more money than the U.S. Treasury then held—much of the 530 million acres acquired was in private hands.

In 1820, only 814,000 acres of public land were put up for sale. At intervals, however, Washington issued land scrip in lieu of cash payments to soldiers. Although fully negotiable, this form of currency nearly always circulated below its face value, for it was pegged to the price of land.

Although some frontiersmen and most speculators grumbled that a lot of good land was being given away by the government, few people not holding high office knew the extent of this practice. During the twenty-year period between 1818 and 1838, the nation granted four hundred thousand acres to entrepreneurs who planned to make river improvements. With a network of canals viewed as the transportation infrastructure of the future, more than a million acres of public land went to capitalists who hoped to dig navigable ditches. Nearly all of these canals were scheduled to be built in the most heavily populated areas of the East.

The free-handed use of public land inevitably drove up the price of what was left. Wealthy speculators—among whom Lamar may have been numbered—bought land scrip at a discount, then used it to make big purchases at official prices.

In cities such as Mobile and New Orleans, scrip and the land it represented had soared to fifty cents per acre by the time the Republic of Texas was established in 1836. Profits from land speculation were so high that Texas scrip began circulating in England, where it brought one shilling per acre.

It was the lure of cheap land that enticed Connecticut-born Moses Austin from Virginia to Spanish Louisiana in 1797. Jefferson's purchase of the region in which Austin lived, soon to become Missouri, led Austin to look west to a region in which he could double or triple his assets quickly. He seems to have had an expedition to Spanish Texas in the planning stages when every man of means was hit hard by the Panic of 1819.

In a letter, Austin confided: "I found nothing I could do would bring back my property again, and to remain in a state of poverty in a Country where I had enjoyed wealth I could not endure." He tried to estimate how much money he could make by securing a land grant in Texas and then charging fees to immigrants for his help in settling there.

Moses Austin was responsible for leading "the Old Three Hundred" settlers into Texas.

DICTIONARY OF AMERICAN PORTRAITS

He could recoup his fortune, Austin believed, if only he could scrape up enough money to get to the faraway Mexican state where there was abundant land to be had. Moses visited his son Stephen, then a district judge in Little Rock, and secured a loan from him. After purchasing a horse, a pack mule, and a slave, the elder Austin still had fifty dollars in cash in hand—more than enough for the envisioned move to Texas.

With the progress of his journey hampered only by the speed of his animals, Moses set out for Natchitoches, Louisiana, the eastern terminus of a four-hundred-mile road to the provincial capital of Texas, San Antonio de Bexar. Austin arrived in San Antonio on December 23, 1820.

With the help of a Dutchman whom he had known in Louisiana, Moses gained the ear of high-ranking officials. If they would grant him two hundred thousand acres, he would function as an *empresario*. In that role, he promised to bring three hundred families and establish an American colony in the sparsely settled region.

When his application was approved, the fifty-three-year-old Moses exulted as he calculated that his fees—sixty dollars per family—would soar to eighteen thousand dollars in three or four years. Although travel-worn and sick, he wrote to his son glowingly: "Raise your spirits. Times are changing and a new chance presents itself." Then he informed him that a delegation of Mexican officials would meet Stephen at Natchitoches in a few weeks to plan transportation for the settlers.

Three weeks after penning these encouraging words, Moses died, possibly of pneumonia. On June 26, 1821, Stephen reluctantly decided that duty required him to assume his father's place in the venture. To do so would require a lengthy move, but he was accustomed to changes of residence.

Born in the region of Virginia where lead mines abound, five-year-old Stephen had moved with his family to Missouri. Since his father was prosperous, the young man was sent to school in Connecticut for three years, after which Stephen studied for two years at Transylvania University in Lexington, Kentucky. Rejoining his family in Missouri, he moved to Arkansas with them and stayed there a time before going to New Orleans to study law.

In 1821 Stephen moved to Mexico's province of Texas, whose independence from Spain had just been gained. Austin invested in a crude printing job, and his advertisement flyer, which he sent back to the United States, made glowing promises. Anyone who would pay the fees and immigrate to his colony would receive a square mile of land (640 acres). Additional land would be awarded to settlers bringing their families.

In the land-hungry East, Austin's offer looked too good to turn down. Scores of city dwellers and a handful of frontiersmen responded, saying they would probably accept it as soon as he sent word for them to come.

Austin was working as a land agent of the Mexican government, having renounced his U.S. citizenship. Reflecting upon this radical course of action later, he wrote to a friend, "I bid an everlasting farewell to my native country, and adopted this [Mexico], and in so doing I determined to fulfill rigidly all the duties and obligations of a Mexican citizen."

With numerous favorable responses to his advertisement in hand, Austin was authorized to offer each settler who came

with his family (with or without children) a league of land—
4,428 acres. Such settlers were obligated to pay $200, but that
could be done in installments.

Austin boosted his request for land from two hundred thousand acres to ten million acres and expected swift acceptance
of the new terms he was now allowed to offer officially. A few
immigrants had not waited for the formal terms of settlement
and had already arrived, and many more were en route. Austin
managed to negotiate permits for 900 families to immigrate,
and about 750 of these arrived in Texas before his last contract
expired in 1834. Under the terms of an 1824 statute, all immigrants were required to renounce their foreign citizenship and
become Mexican citizens.

Texas's first official census, taken in 1825, certified a population of 1,800, of whom 443 were slaves. Six years later the
population had more than tripled to 5,666.

Far from being a lone land agent, Austin competed with
numerous other *empresarios*. One of them was Georgia-born
Mirabeau B. Lamar, who persuaded friends and relatives to let
him invest six thousand dollars for them. He purchased eleven
leagues of land but never filled this tract with colonists.

In fact, none of Austin's competitors rivaled his success, so
he is considered the "father" of Texas. Stressing that personal
gain was not his chief motivation, he wrote: "My ambition has
been to succeed in redeeming Texas from its wilderness state
by means of the plough alone, in spreading over it a North
American population [filled with] enterprise and intelligence.
In doing this I hoped to make the fortunes of thousands, and
my own among the rest."

Formerly a separate province, Texas was now merged with
the Mexican state of Coahuila, and its capital was established
at Saltillo. A provincial constitution was adopted in 1827. Three
years later, further immigration by Americans was forbidden,
but unscrupulous *empresarios* continued to sell thousands of
scrip certificates to prospective settlers who did not realize that
their purchases did not convey titles to land but only gave
them permission to settle on the land.

The leadership of the Mexican government had been in turmoil throughout the years following Mexico's independence
from Spain, but in 1833 the hero of the revolution, Gen. Antonio López de Santa Anna, was elected president. Santa Anna,

however, interpreted his powers freely and became more a dictator than a president.

Meanwhile, American immigration to the Texas colonies proceeded briskly. By 1830 there were significant settlements at Brazoria, Washington-on-the-Brazos, San Felipe de Austin, Anahuac, and Gonzales. Two problems began to disturb the Americans' Mexican neighbors. One was that Mexican citizenship required conversion to Roman Catholicism, a requirement that most Americans ignored. The second problem was that the Americans were beginning to outnumber the Mexicans by a ratio of almost three to one. In response to these developments, the Mexican government closed the border and suspended American immigration. These steps were temporary, due to political upheavals in Mexico City, but the ascension to power of Santa Anna quickly settled the matter.

In 1834 the American settlers petitioned Santa Anna for statehood for Texas and sent Austin to Mexico City with their requests. The *empresario* negotiated with some success, but statehood for Texas was not possible. When Austin started to return, he was accused of treason and arrested. During eighteen months of incarceration, the pioneer concluded that Texans could only defend their rights by force of arms.

The Texas Revolution began in 1835, when Mexican troops attempted to disarm the American colony at Gonzales. The Texans then drove the Mexican army from the region through a series of surprise attacks. Delegates from a dozen settlements gathered at San Felipe de Austin and voted to fight for the rights they believed had been guaranteed by the Mexican Constitution of 1824. Santa Anna, however, was in no mood to negotiate. He led the army back to Texas to crush the rebellion.

At Washington-on-the-Brazos, Texas declared its independence on March 2, 1836. Meanwhile, Santa Anna's army confronted stubborn resistance in San Antonio at the Texas garrison known as the Alamo. The garrison was overrun, and no prisoners were taken. Later, the Mexican army massacred several hundred Texans who had been captured in an attack on Goliad. Santa Anna then divided his army to cover the vast areas of American settlement. The small Texas army drew Santa Anna's force into the bayous near the site of present-day Houston. On April 21, 1836, the Texans surprised the Mexican force at San Jacinto and captured Santa Anna.

An artist's conception of early Austin, Texas, with the capitol of the republic at upper left.

Austin was alone among prominent Texans in opposing the death penalty for Santa Anna. That stand may have been one of the prime reasons why he failed to be elected the first president of the new republic, losing that office to Sam Houston by an overwhelming majority in September 1836.

Austin instead became Houston's secretary of state, but he held that office for only a few months. In December 1836 the land agent whose efficient work made him the Father of Texas died at the age of forty-three. He did see Austin County created on March 17, 1836, around present-day Bellville. Launched as San Felipe de Austin, the city grew up from the first permanent settlement of Americans in Texas.

In 1839 the Texas legislature selected a site in Travis County for the republic's capital and chose to name it after the man who had opened the door for American colonization of the region known as Texas. Austin has continued to be the capital of Texas to the modern day.

2

Samuel P. Colt

The Texas Revolver

The Texas Rangers had been founded in 1835 during the Texas Revolution. Principally, they were organized to protect the frontier settlers from the Native American population. Said to "ride like Mexicans, shoot like Tennesseans, and fight like the devil," the Rangers were a unique police force. They wore no uniform, never drilled, and were not required to salute their officers. In time the only distinguishing element of the Ranger would be his weapon.

Scruffy in appearance, lean and lank because of much hard riding and little good food, several Rangers stood at—what passed for them as—attention. John Coffee Hays, formerly of Tennessee, had been ordered to increase the size of his force to 150 men and to patrol the region between the San Antonio River and the Rio Grande. Since the fledgling Texas government had no money with which to pay the Rangers, Hays was finding recruitment slow.

Some of the men called spies by Mexican Gen. Adrian Woll mumbled audibly, wondering what on Earth Cap'n Jack had in mind. They rarely assembled at headquarters, so calling a mass meeting made some wonder whether their leader might have some advance word of a Comanche raid or some other catastrophe.

Hays wasted no words. Without speaking, he drew his battered pistol from his belt and tossed it casually in the general direction of a pile of trash. Before his astonished followers could ask what possessed him to do a thing like that, he reached behind his back and pulled out a shiny new weapon.

Flourishing it by its barrel, he addressed his discarded pistol, "Bye-bye, Old-timer!"

The Rangers, who had wondered whether Hays had been eating peyote, were then given a brief introduction to the weapon that had arrived by stagecoach the previous day. A fellow back East, name of Colt, had gone into manufacturing, Hays explained. He was making something new—a pistol with a revolving chamber that held five cartridges.

Demonstrating the movement of the gun's parts—clumsy and slow by comparison with later models—Hayes allowed as how he was itching to meet a band of Comanches or Mexicans. With his foes within range, he would get off five shots "in less time than it takes to reload Old Betsy over there," and he gestured toward his discarded single-shot pistol.

Hays's men were not convinced by what they heard and saw. Some of them had tangled with Comanches, and they knew how these plains Indians fought. Slipping from the back of his horse, an experienced warrior was protected by hanging over the animal's far side. Waiting until the Rangers had emptied their pistols, the Comanche shot beneath the neck of his horse and could get off half a dozen arrows in the time it took to reload a pistol.

Sensing uncertainty on the part of his men, some of whom had been in his company only a few days, Hays lifted the pistol and pointed upward. He fired five times in rapid succession and muttered, "Waste of ammunition. Any fool with a stiff trigger finger can empty this little beauty in thirty seconds!"

Most of the Rangers stationed at San Antonio during 1842–43 managed to scrape together enough money to get five-shooters of their own. During the hot weather of 1844, Hays and fifteen of his men, all armed with Colts, were attacked by a band of Comanches on the banks of the Pedernales River. Every time the Comanches charged, thinking the Rangers had emptied their guns or were reloading, they rode into a fresh volley. Although the Comanches outnumbered the Rangers nearly six to one, half of the attackers were casualties by the time the engagement was over.

After that celebrated incident, so many Rangers and civilians sent orders to Samuel F. Colt that in the East his revolutionary weapon came to be known as "the Texas Colt." It

Samuel P. Colt.

H WRIGHT SMITH ENGRAVING, NEW YORK PUBLIC LIBRARY

appeared to the youthful inventor briefly that he was on the way to prosperity—thanks to Captain Jack and his Rangers.

A Connecticut Yankee born in Hartford, Colt began his career at the age of ten when he went to work in his father's silk mill at Ware, Massachusetts. He had tried school, but two years were enough; to his father, whose business had failed, he announced that he was going to sea.

On the brig *Corvo*, the young Colt reached London and then Calcutta before sailing home. Tradition has it that on the return voyage, fascinated by the way the ship's windlass turned, Colt had a sudden inspiration. With wood scrounged from a split tackle block, he whittled a model of what he called a revolver: a pistol whose chamber revolved around its barrel.

Back in Boston by 1831, the self-styled inventor borrowed enough money to have a couple of revolvers made. One of them, however, exploded, and the other refused to fire. Frustrated, Colt changed careers and spent three years on the lecture circuit. Calling himself "the celebrated Dr. Coult," he charged twenty-five cents to demonstrate the effects of laughing gas (nitrous

Before achieving success as an arms manufacturer, the celebrated "Dr. Coult" sold laughing gas.

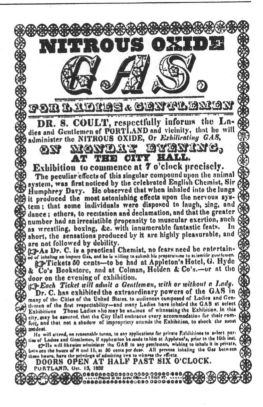

NITROUS OXIDE GAS.

FOR LADIES & GENTLEMEN

DR. S. COULT, respectfully informs the La-
dies and Gentlemen of PORTLAND and vicinity, that he will
administer the NITROUS OXIDE, Or *Exhilirating GAS,*

ON MONDAY EVENING,
AT THE CITY HALL.

Exhibition to commence at **7** o'clock precisely.

The peculiar effects of this singular compound upon the animal
system, was first noticed by the celebrated English Chemist, Sir
Humphrey Davy. He observed that when inhaled into the lungs
it produced the most astonishing effects upon the nervous system; that some individuals were disposed to laugh, sing, and
dance; others, to recitation and declamation, and that the greater
number had an irresistible propensity to muscular exertion, such
as wrestling, boxing, &c. with innumerable fantastic feats. In
short, the sensations produced by it are highly pleasurable, and
are not followed by debility.

☞As Dr. C. is a practical Chemist, no fears need be entertain-
ed of inhaling an impure Gas, and he is willing to submit his preparations to scientific gentlemen.

☞Tickets 50 cents—to be had at Appleton's Hotel, G. Hyde
& Co's Bookstore, and at Colman, Holden & Co's.—or at the
door on the evening of exhibition.

☞*Each Ticket will admit a Gentleman, with or without a Lady.*

Dr. C. has exhibited the extraordinary powers of the GAS in
many of the Cities of the United States, to audiences composed of Ladies and Gentlemen of the first respectability—and many Ladies have inhaled the GAS at select
Exhibitions. Those Ladies who may be anxious of witnessing the Exhibition, in this
city, may be assured, that the City Hall embraces every accommodation for their comfort, and that not a shadow of impropriety attends the Exhibition, to shock the most
modest.

He will attend, on reasonable terms, to any applications for private Exhibitions to select parties of Ladies and Gentlemen, if application be made to him at Appleton's, prior to the 10th inst.

☞He will likewise administer the GAS to any gentleman, wishing to inhale it in private,
between the hours of 8 and 11, at 50 cents per dose. All persons inhaling the Gas between
these hours, have the privilege of admitting two to witness the effects.

DOORS OPEN AT HALF PAST SIX O'CLOCK.
PORTLAND, Oct. 13, 1832

oxide), which later was used in dentistry as one of the first
anesthetics.

Colt saved sufficient money to return to work on his revolving pistol. He secured patents in England and France before
receiving U.S. Patent 138, signed by President Andrew Jackson
and Secretary of War Benjamin F. Butler. Always a smooth
talker, Colt then persuaded wealthy investors to put up the
money to build a revolver factory. Like Colt, these men
expected to make a quick fortune from sales to the U.S. Army.

The top officials at the Ordnance Department in Washington
City were not interested, however. They had plenty of
breechloading muskets and flintlock pistols, with armories
producing new ones every week. When Colt managed to get
one of his percussion-type weapons into a shooting match at
West Point, experienced officers scorned the revolver as
"entirely too complicated for use in combat." During five years

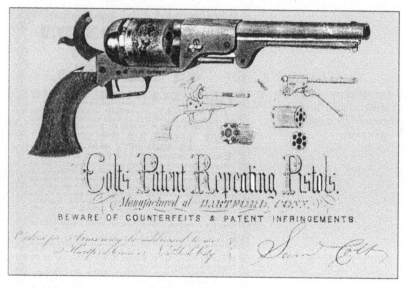

Colt's patented repeating pistol, widely known as "the Patterson," as depicted in broadsides of the 1850s.

of labored selling, Colt managed to sell only two hundred of his weapons, so he declared bankruptcy in 1842.

Still fascinated with weapons, the inventor at whom nearly everyone laughed next developed what he called a submarine: an underwater explosive device that could be triggered electronically from shore. Although he gave a successful demonstration, the U.S. Navy was not interested.

Working with Samuel F. B. Morse, Colt devised a waterproof insulation so that telegraph wires could function under water. Yet despite some minor successes in a variety of endeavors, during a period of thirty or so months, Colt's only weapons sales were of ammunition that he sold very cheaply.

Colt's turnaround came after he sent one of his revolvers to Jack Hays. With the profits from his Texas sales and other remote places, Colt adapted a revolutionary idea by Eli Whitney and began producing weapons with interchangeable parts. This cut production cost drastically and made even two or three segments of a damaged pistol worth something to a repair shop.

Samuel Colt's weapons were prominently displayed in New York at the Crystal Palace Exposition of 1853.

With a war with Mexico looming, Ranger Capt. Samuel H. Walker drafted a letter to the revolver manufacturer. In it the experienced Indian fighter praised the Texas Colt but said that it needed improvement and at least one more cartridge chamber. He added: "With improvements, I think [Colt's five-shot revolvers] can be rendered into the most perfect weapon in the World for light mounted troops. Throughout Texas, people are anxious to get [their hands on] your pistols."

Acting on Walker's suggestion, Colt designed a new and heavier model that held six .44-caliber cartridges. When the first pair of his new pistols came off the assembly line, the inventor shipped them to Texas. Sam Houston had approved Walker's order for one thousand "Walker Colts." Relayed to their purchaser, who by then was fighting in Mexico, the improved weapons reached Walker a few days before he was killed in action.

Colt dispatched a letter of gratitude to Houston, saying: "I am truly plesed to lern that your influance, unasked for by a poor

Colt built a mansion and called it Armsmear.

devil of an inventor, has from your sense of what is right been
employed to du away with prejudice [against revolving pistols]."

The Texas Rangers and the Mexican War elevated the
weapons into prominence. With the coming of civil war to the
United States, Colt's business boomed so rapidly that he built a
huge factory and a costly mansion. His successors who operated the factory produced dozens of new models, all of which
they labeled as "greatly improved." One model became famous
as the Peacemaker, or "the six-shooter that won the West."

Nearly a decade before the Peacemaker appeared, Samuel
Colt died at the age of forty-eight. Except for Presidents
Andrew Jackson, John Tyler, and James K. Polk, the Connecticut Yankee influenced early Texas more than any other man
who never set foot upon its soil. It was not long before many
had heard the saying that God may have made all men, but
Samuel Colt made them equal. Thus the one distinctive element of the Texas Rangers came to be that they all wore Colts
at their side.

3

Babe Didrikson

One-Woman Team

It is said that Virginia Van Wie and Betty Jameson, two great golfers, were sitting in the courtyard of a country club in 1945. They were absorbed with plans to resume the U.S. Women's Amateur Golf Tournament, which had been suspended during World War II. Van Wie had taken top honors in the prestigious event three times, and Jameson was a two-time winner who had high hopes for 1946. Van Wie remarked that her friend had better practice diligently, as she had heard that Babe Didrikson of Texas, who had made her name in the 1932 Olympics, planned to compete.

Laughter was the only response to the warning. Most women who played golf in those days came from wealthy backgrounds. It seemed ridiculous to think that a woman from a low-income family could be a serious contender in a national tournament of female golfers.

Babe Didrikson Zaharias would be thirty-two years old in 1946. Until age eighteen, she never held a golf club, and with such a late start, her potential rivals did not consider her a serious threat.

Born in Port Arthur, Mildred "Babe" Didrikson moved with her family to Beaumont at age three. A swing hanging from the limb of a tree in the yard of her home on Doucette Street was her favorite place during early childhood. Often scolded for acting like a tomboy, she was both agile and strong. After a visit to a traveling circus, Babe constructed a trapeze of her own, using broomsticks as bars to form its seat.

As she grew older, one of Babe's favorite activities was jumping hedges as she dashed through the neighbors' yards. Her father, a Norwegian carpenter, was not greatly surprised when he learned that his fourteen-year-old daughter was named captain of a football team. "Babe can do just about anything she wants to do," he often said.

As a high school freshman she badly wanted to make the girls' basketball team, and she easily replaced a junior in the coveted spot. On the court, she handled the ball so deftly that word of her prowess reached an insurance company in Dallas. Hence M. J. McCombs, head of the company's athletic program for female employees, drove to Beaumont to see Babe play.

At the half, he offered the fifteen-year-old a job and a place on the company basketball team. Her parents were delighted that she had been given such a good opportunity and said they would come to see her at every opportunity. Neither Babe nor her parents then anticipated that she would soon be training for the 1930 Amateur Athletic Union meet in Chicago.

In a letter home, the girl who was beginning to be the talk of Dallas reported casually that, in the city's softball league, she had hit thirteen runs in a double-header contest. Although McCombs had brought Babe to Dallas to play basketball, he quickly found that one sport did not exhaust all of her energy. In addition to softball, she was soon heavily involved in diving, swimming, and was giving exhibitions on how to handle a speedboat.

When McCombs took Babe to Chicago for the AAU track and field meet, Babe was a bit taken aback to discover that teams of twelve to twenty-five girls would participate in some events. Having no colleagues, the representative of the Employers Casualty Company was called by Chicago sportswriters "the one-girl team from Dallas."

Babe entered the discus throw—an event in which she had no experience—as well as the shot put, javelin throw, broad jump, high jump, hurdles, and two other events. She not only qualified for the upcoming Olympic Games in Los Angeles but also set world records in the 80-meter hurdles and the javelin throw.

The men who made up the International Olympic Committee (IOC) were ultraconservative in their views concerning female athletes. Baron Pierre de Coubertin, a founder of the modern games, once told a reporter, "It is indecent that the spectators should be exposed to the risk of seeing the body of

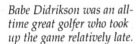

Babe Didrikson was an all-time great golfer who took up the game relatively late.

BEAUMONT CONVENTION AND VISITORS BUREAU

a woman being smashed before their eyes. Besides, no matter how toughened a sportswoman may be, her organism is not cut out to sustain certain shocks." Therefore the IOC had refused to permit a woman from Greece to compete in the first marathon race in 1896.

In 1928 Elizabeth Robinson of the United States, Halina Konopacka of Poland, and Lina Radke and Ethel Catherwood of Germany had demonstrated that women could excel in track and field events. Their prowess persuaded officials to include in the 1932 Olympic games two new events for women: the javelin throw and the 80-meter hurdles.

While training in California, Babe learned of the additional events. She won both of them, setting world records. She failed to take the gold medal in the high jump only because she used the then unorthodox Western roll in winning.

Feted as a national heroine, she celebrated by taking up golf. She played her first game with the noted sportswriter Grantland Rice, who urged her to give up fencing, tennis, billiards, and boxing to concentrate on golf. "It will be a long and hard journey to the top in golf," he warned. "You will be competing with women who have been playing for years."

Babe practiced diligently and in 1934 felt that she was ready to try her skill against others. Entering a Fort Worth tournament, she shot a 77 and won a medal. That encouraged her to enter the Texas State Women's Golf Tournament a few months later. Again, she won handily.

Devoting a great deal of time and energy to the golf circuit, in 1938 Babe took part in the Los Angeles Open. There she drew wrestler George Zaharias as a partner, and she soon said yes when he proposed marriage.

When the U.S. Women's Amateur Tournament resumed in 1946, Babe Didrikson Zaharias was there. That's when she won her first national championship, after which she went on to become the first woman from the United States to win the British Women's Amateur Golf Tournament.

Records show that "Mrs. M. D. Zaharias" was the first U.S. Women's Open champion in 1948. Called the world champion of women's golf for four consecutive years—1948, 1949, 1950, and 1951—she lost the U.S. Women's Open to Louise Suggs in 1949 but took the title again in 1950.

Stricken by cancer in 1953, Babe Didrikson was described by sports commentators as "having been eliminated from competition in the prime of life." She beat the odds, however, and made a comeback in 1954, winning the U.S. Women's Open for the third time. Her place among all-time great women golfers was assured.

In 1950 the Associated Press named her the outstanding woman athlete of the first half of the twentieth century. That accolade, many say, is inadequate to describe a woman who died in 1956 at the age of forty-two. Her admirers cite statistics to buttress their claim that the Texan was the finest female athlete who ever lived.

4

Gail Borden

Lucky Dabbler

M̲en who travel long distances across uninhabited country must get mighty hungry," Penelope Borden mused one night after supper.

"Most of them are good hunters," her husband responded. "They can live off the land most of the time." Pausing and wrinkling his forehead because he was hit by a sudden thought, he turned to his wife and admitted, "Some of them must have it hard, part of the time."

That conversation turned the versatile mind of Gail Borden toward the idea of preserving food without refrigeration. After all, he reasoned, his father had preserved the sap of maple trees by boiling it until it turned into syrup. Why not do the same thing with meat?

After building a work shed, the would-be inventor boiled some meat until all the water evaporated, but the meat soon turned rank. He tried baking, which did not produce the results he wanted. He turned to drying small particles in the sun. These did not spoil, but they were so tough no one could chew them.

Eventually Borden developed a product that he hoped he could market successfully. After boiling a side of beef until it had shrunk to a few pounds, he mixed the condensed meat with flour. Molded in the form of biscuits and baked until brown, the foodstuff kept for many weeks without spoiling, was not chewy, and remained edible.

Although he went to London's 1851 Crystal Palace Exposition to exhibit "the wonderful meat biscuit from Texas," actual purchasers remained few. If Borden expected a financial wind-fall with his meat biscuit, the inventor would have to improve its taste and find an economical way to produce it in quantity. Borden had already invented a water pump and a crude ice box in which food could be stored, but these devices were not successful either. He then spent several months tinkering with a wagon that did not require horses or mules. Wind-powered by a large sail, Borden's "terraqueous machine" moved fast when the wind was high and could be steered by a mechanism similar to those on many boats. A public demonstration came to a disastrous halt, however, when his contraption veered into a lake and sank.

When his friends and acquaintances laughed at his hope of becoming a noted inventor, Borden said little. After all, he rea-soned, his experiences were a lot more varied than those of most early Texans.

Borden had taken the trail west in 1829 at the age of twenty-eight. After spending his boyhood in New York, he had gone with his parents to Kentucky and to Indiana. Then, like other restless men of his era, he moved on his own, first to Missis-sippi for seven years and then he heard about Stephen F. Austin's colony in Texas.

During his travels, Borden had become a skilled surveyor, and surveyors were scarce in Texas. Acquiring four thousand acres of land and settling at San Felipe de Austin, he was soon in charge of the land office. An early acquaintance, Noah Smithwick, recalled that when Borden first entered the Ameri-can colony in Texas, he made his living as a blacksmith. Later Borden compiled the first topographical map of the state.

Just four years after having crossed the Mississippi River, Borden was a delegate to the 1833 convention that assembled to present the colony's grievances to the Mexican government. There was little doubt that the delegates to this conference were rebellious, for they framed a constitution designed to change things in the Mexican province of Texas. Six delegates signed an open challenge to Mexican president Antonio López de Santa Anna. If necessary, they wrote, all Texans should make ready to defend their rights by force of arms.

By 1835 Borden had put aside his surveying instruments and record books and had begun to publish a newspaper in part-nership with his brother Thomas. Together they issued the *Tele-*

Explorer Elisha Kane took Borden's meat biscuits with him to the Arctic.

THOMAS PHILLIBROWNE ENGRAVING

graph and Texas Land Register, the first newspaper in the Lone Star State. During the revolt against Mexico, the *Telegraph,* which was moved to Houston after Santa Anna's men destroyed the press, had a monopoly of sorts, since there were no competitors.

As a reward for his services during the revolution, President Sam Houston appointed Borden the collector of customs for the port of Galveston. From that post he moved up and took charge of the Galveston City Company, making him a prototype of today's city manager.

It was in Galveston that he finally perfected his meat biscuit, hoping that U.S. Army quartermasters and immigrants headed toward California would become customers. Although that did not happen, he was pleased when he received a request to provide a supply of meat biscuits—which some had begun to call "pemmican"—for an Arctic expedition led by Elisha Kane in 1851.

Kane's endorsement of the product was good publicity, but it too failed to generate significant sales. Borden was heavily

UNITED SOCIETY OF SHAKERS, SABBATHDAY LAKE, MAINE

A vacuum pan evaporator, probably invented by Brother Alonzo Hollister of Maine, was the key to Borden's success in producing condensed milk.

in debt for the equipment used to mass produce the meat biscuits. Thus he declared bankruptcy and left town to avoid his creditors.

Arriving in New York, he devoted his attention to the problem of preserving milk. Nothing that he tried worked; the milk continued to sour regardless of the variety of ways Borden devised for processing it.

During a visit to a Shaker community, he saw farmers using what some of them called a "vacuum pan"—a tank from which they had removed most of the air. Fruit preserved in such a pan, the Shakers explained, remained sweet for months.

Elated, Borden soon tested the pan with milk, finding that the milk in the pan would boil at a temperature barely more than half that normally required. Since the Shakers and others who preserved fruit added sugar to the syrup, Borden decided to do so with milk. At last he was successful, and the sweetened milk that had been boiled in the vacuum pan retained a good taste and offered a long shelf life. Borden's next step was to apply for a patent, which was rejected without explanation. It took him many months to convince the Patent Office that he had developed a process that was both original and useful. When Patent 15,553 was finally awarded him in 1856, he borrowed money to open a plant in Connecticut to produce what Borden now called condensed milk. His machinery worked well, but his neighbors, who were accustomed to fresh milk from their own cows, were reluctant to try Borden's condensed milk.

Borden refused to accept a negative verdict and built a two-wheeled cart, taking his condensed milk to the streets of New York City. His sales were not sufficient to keep the plant in operation, but Borden met wealthy Jeremiah Milbank and persuaded him to advance him enough money to pay his debts.

Solvent once more, the inventor believed that his condensed milk was precisely what the U.S. Army needed. The military tasted his milk, saw that it could be used after many weeks, and agreed that it might be useful. Just now, however, the troops did not need it because plenty of fresh milk was available near the army posts.

The Civil War brought a dramatic change in military thinking. Only about sixteen thousand men made up the U.S. Army in 1861, but soon the number doubled and continued to grow. Condensed milk was seen as a way to help keep fighting men healthy, and Union officials contracted to purchase all that could be manufactured.

Like Thomas Edison, Gail Borden has been called a lucky dabbler whose persistence enabled him to stumble upon a great invention. Both men were self-taught, and both were looked upon somewhat scornfully by many trained scientists. Yet Borden and Edison both effected radical changes in the way of life of their fellow citizens. Noah Smithwick, whose memory is the only authority for the fact that Borden was once a blacksmith, gloated in his old age that his friend's Eagle brand condensed milk had become "a feature of every grocery store and every advertising medium" in the nation.

Returning to his beloved Texas as a rich and famous man, Gail Borden never stopped trying to develop new ways to process foodstuffs. He acquired a patent for his method of

Gail Borden, after his return to his beloved Texas as a world-renowned inventor.

DICTIONARY OF AMERICAN PORTRAITS

"concentrating cider and other juices and fruits" and found a way to produce an extract of beef that many housewives praised. He succeeded in condensing tea, cocoa, and coffee—coming close to producing an instant coffee and instant tea.

Two years before his death at age seventy-three, Texas lawmakers honored the pioneer Texan by creating Borden County from the Bexar District. South of Lubbock, the town of Gail is today the county seat of the region to which Gail Borden returned after having helped to win the Civil War with a product that no one wanted initially.

5

Waylon Jennings

Platinum Outlaw

Jessie Colter, also known as Mrs. Waylon Jennings, was disgusted with one of her songs and decided to trash it. "No use to keep trying," she said. "It's sorta silly—and has no rhyme at all."

Her husband, who by the late 1970s was known for doing the unexpected, nodded understanding. As soon as Jessie's back was turned, however, he rescued the song and eventually persuaded her to sing it with him. Their duet, "Storms Never Last," was produced by Richie Albright and was later seen as a sign that the storms that had beset Waylon were about to give way to clear skies.

Two decades earlier, the instrumentalist, composer, and singer had reason to wonder what unseen force was watching over him. Buddy Holly and his reorganized Crickets trio had played Clear Lake, Iowa, on February 2, 1959. Their next stop was Moorhead, Minnesota. Everyone was exhausted.

Holly, who ordinarily did not do so, chartered a plane to take him, Jennings, and Tommy Allsup to Fargo, North Dakota—not far from their ultimate destination. Close to take-off time, a pair of rock stars who were considered minor celebrities bribed the owner of the little plane to give them two of its three passenger seats.

Flipping a coin to decide who would fly and who would make the long and tiresome bus trip, Tommy Allsup and twenty-one-year-old Jennings lost. As they stood on the tarmac cursing their bad luck and watching the little plane disappear into the distance, they never thought that it would crash as soon as it was out of sight. When the aircraft plowed into a cornfield less than ten miles from Mason City, the pilot, Buddy Holly, Ritchie Valens, and J. P. "The Big Bopper" Richardson were killed.

The tragedy inspired a Don McLean song ten years later with the line "The day the music died." Long before that song was released, a wrung-out bass player had hightailed it to Lubbock and was back at radio station KLLL, which he felt was a safe haven after the crash he barely missed.

Born in 1937 in Littlefield, not far from Lubbock, a boy with both Comanche and Cherokee heritages later called his hometown "the outskirts of a cotton patch." By the time Waylon was old enough to hold a bag on his shoulder he began picking cotton and then picking his twangy guitar to forget his aching back and sore fingers. When he wasn't listening to country music from Nashville's clear-signal station, he sang a lot of his own compositions and tried to sound like Jimmie Rodgers. When he wasn't in a Rodgers mood, he imitated Ernest Tubb.

Picking and singing brought him his own radio, as first prize in a contest sponsored by radio station KSEL. Winning that radio was like hitting the jackpot at Monte Carlo, only more so. Waylon dropped out of school and wangled his way into one talent show after another. By the time he was fourteen, he had landed a fifteen-minute spot on KSEL as a home-grown country singer.

A little later, after he had cut out for Lubbock and landed a job at its country–rock 'n' roll radio station, the eighteen-year-old guitarist, songwriter, and singer thought he had hit the big time. He made friends with Buddy Holly, who was producing under the Brunswick label, and cut his first record for him. One side, a tried-and-tested favorite called "Jole Blon" required Waylon to sing phonetically, since he didn't know Cajun French. Although the record was not a good seller, Holly persuaded his protégé to play bass with his Crickets.

Back in Lubbock after the plane crash, with lots of memories of Holly, Waylon was restless. He left Texas for Phoenix, landing at D.J.'s and Wild Bill's, a club that attracted a wide clientele ranging from doctors, lawyers, and store clerks to cowboys and housewives. Facing those audiences, Jennings began experimenting with playing pop tunes in a country style. A live

LES LEVERETT

Waylon Jennings made music history by rendering his own compositions in his own style.

recording made at the club featured "Abilene" and somewhat eased his homesickness for Texas.

Almost as soon as he put together his own band, The Waylors, Waylon began cutting records for Herb Alpert of A&M Records. One of his buddies was constantly writing letters about how great Jennings was to Chet Atkins, an RCA producer in Nashville. Finally the bombardment of mail paid off. In 1965 Waylon was given a contract that took him to Nashville.

His first album for RCA, *Folk Country*, was supported by Loretta Lynn, Tex Ritter, and Porter Wagoner and included some of his own compositions. It didn't take the man from Littlefield long to hit the top ten, and by 1969 he took home a Grammy award.

Life should have been all peaches and cream, but it wasn't. Lonely and bitter after the breakup of a marriage, Jennings teamed with Johnny Cash in his free time, and the two of them tried to see who could outdo the other in "wild man, really wild" living.

Part of his trouble, Waylon realized at the time and admitted later, stemmed from his increasingly frequent clashes with the recording industry in Nashville. "I had always wanted to do music my way, instead of somebody else's way," he recalled later. "The business of laying down four songs in three hours—all of 'em clearly marked with 'the Nashville sound'—was just too much for me." In spite of the frustration that gnawed at him every time he walked into a studio, he managed to turn out three consecutive number-one singles—not just once, but twice.

In 1978 he didn't realize that his life was about to make a right turn when he recorded "Don't You Think This Outlaw Bit's Done Got Out of Hand," which was based on the sudden move into his life of a drug squad. Hank Williams Jr. was in the studio the night that classic was cut, and he may have been the first person to label Waylon "an outlaw from the Grand Ole Opry tradition."

Whether that's the case or not, the man whose first guitar was from Gene Autry's line of merchandise turned his back on Nashville radio station WSM, after a fashion. With Willie Nelson egging him on, Waylon shed his fancy outfits and quit greasing his hair. He took to wearing jeans like his father back in Littlefield and put on leather boots and some turquoise jewelry.

Lots of admirers believe that his album *Dreaming My Dreams* is the best album he ever turned out. Few of his songs, though, are so autobiographical as "Are You Sure Hank Done It This Way?" The memorable start of that album delineates a still-insightful look at the stagnation that prevailed in the country music industry at the time.

Although Kris Kristofferson was also deeply involved, it was Waylon, more than any other individual, who made country music turn its back on musical baby food. As a team with Willie Nelson, the two became "Waylie" and made more musical history than they had anticipated.

By 1973 Waylon had stopped taking orders from anyone; he had full artistic control of the album *Honky Tonk Heroes*. Having been jerked out of lethargy by "Black Rose," he used it as the opener of the album. Hailed as innovative throughout the nation and abroad, his rendition contained the personal lines: "The Devil made me do it the first time. / The second time around I done it on my own."

Waylon and Willie joined forces the following year to co-produce the album *This Time*, featuring as its title song a composition by the man who thought he had hit the top when he had his own radio show in Lubbock. Before the end of 1974, Jennings was the sole producer of the album *Waylon, The Ramblin' Man*. Never forgetting his roots, he had "Luckenbach, Texas" almost ready to release when he heard a rumor that both New York and Nashville might soon be due for a surprise. Sure enough, *Wanted: The Outlaws* turned out to be the first platinum album to come from Nashville.

A diabetic who has to stay off alcohol and watch his intake of carbohydrates, Jennings tries to avoid social situations that draw photographers, and he seldom gives interviews. With surprisingly broad interests, he serves along with scholar Gabor Boritt, author Shelby Foote, and producer Ken Burns as a member of the national advisory board for the U.S. Civil War Center in Baton Rouge.

It does not bother the outlaw who was the first country musician to hit platinum that such an achievement does not square with his own characterization of his performances: "My music ain't no Nashville sound. It's just my own kind of country—not western, but Waylon."

6
Ann Richards
Out But Not Down

"Poor George . . . he can't help it that he was born with a silver foot in his mouth!" That one-liner, the highlight of the keynote address at the 1988 National Democratic Convention in Atlanta, evoked laughter among the delegates and the nationwide television audience.

The speaker, Ann Richards, later stressed that she had not intended to slam the vice president who would be the Republican nominee. "Negative speeches are very hard to carry off," she said, "and they leave [listeners] with a bad taste."

Richards should know. She began facing audiences in adolescence and learned from every encounter. As a member of a high school debate team she discovered that "the audience variable" is often overlooked. Two identical messages, delivered to two separate audiences, won't come off in identical fashion, although many a public speaker overlooks this factor.

The autobiography of Ann Richards is studded with so many observations that it gives better—and much more readable—advice than many textbooks about public speaking. "In a big hall, it helps a lot to have the lights dimmed," she has learned. "Listeners are always likely to become involved in making deals or greeting friends." She prefers to wait until the lights are low before going onstage because "when the only light comes from the stage, they're more likely to listen."

Adept at persuading audiences to listen, then to laugh both at her and at themselves, the former governor of Texas shared good advice:

Gov. Ann Richards proudly posed with a gift Harley-Davidson then presented it to one of her many departments.

Language ought to bind us together, not divide us. If my mama in Waco can't understand what I'm talking about, chances are that no one else can.

Political messages don't have to consist of lofty rhetoric. They can be personal and can provide fun second only to baseball and football.

There's real joy in saying what you actually think; when that's the case, whatever comes out of your mouth is really yours!

Texas is literally the crossroads of America and I'm proud to be part of a state where you can start out on a front porch in Lakeview and end up on the front porch of the governor's mansion.

If you'll give women a chance, we can perform. After all, Ginger Rogers did everything Fred Astaire did. She just did it backwards and in high heels.

I have never quite understood protocol—this business of who goes to see whom, depending upon rank and prestige. I've always thought such posturing was stupid and artificial.

Until very recent times, the most notable female in the annals of Texas was the woman in the Alamo who had sense enough to leave before she got herself killed.

You have to know people in order to know things. People are my sources of information.

Television has its own special set of pitfalls; you're tempted to talk to the camera instead of talking to the people who are watching.

When a CBS television production crew went to Austin to film a documentary about the state's first elected female governor, a staff member reacted negatively to the fast-moving woman who's quick with quips. "She has the tongue of an adder," he said. Former President George Bush does not agree. He laughed at her jibe and sent her a silver pin shaped like a foot, which she wore with pride.

Ann Richards's political career has been based on eagerness to see women and minorities treated "just like white gentlemen who wear starched collars and navy blue suits." Born in the town of Lakeview but reared in Waco, she won a scholarship to Baylor University where she debated at the college level.

Already, she had been introduced to politics by representing Waco at the Texas Girls' State, which was sponsored by the Women's Auxiliary of the American Legion. Participants in this event established a mock government, and two girls who took part in the exercise were selected to go to the nation's capital to experience Girls' Nation. To her surprise, Ann was one of the pair who went to Washington from Texas, and she met President Harry S. Truman.

"That really whetted my appetite," Richards recalled years afterward. "It made me want to throw my hat into the political ring—but I waited awhile, since I then believed that it was impossible for a female to win a statewide office."

When she was a girl, Waco had a black community, but as in thousands of other towns, there was little intermingling with whites. Although Richards strongly believed that "women

were the civilizers of Texas," while earning a teacher's certifi-
cate at the University of Texas in Austin, she was struck by the
realization that women are largely ignored in the history of the
state. Having discovered a cause to which she could give herself without reservation, she took up the task of compiling and
exhibiting Texas history from a woman's viewpoint.

Although she was not aware of it at the time, the "traveling
exhibit about the role of women" nudged her toward a political
career. It was launched by successful service as campaign manager for Sarah Weddington, who campaigned for a seat in the
legislature. Later Richards helped Wilhemina Delco become
the state's first black lawmaker. After serving as a commissioner
of Travis County, she fought and won a personal battle against
alcoholism.

In a 1982 statewide election, Democrat Richards staged an
upset to win the post of treasurer of the Lone Star State. At that
time the treasury office business practices were similar to "the
days when bookkeepers wore eyeshades and sleeve garters."
Records of the multimillion-dollar cigarette tax stamp program, she says, "were kept in a ledger with a number-two lead
pencil." Remittances were processed by hand at the point of
their receipt and were then sent to a regional office after about
a week. Slowly moving up the fiscal pipeline, they reached
Austin for another stop before going to the treasury.

Richards streamlined and modernized procedures, installing
computers, and agents in field offices were told to begin
making daily deposits at a nearby bank. This accelerated the
pace at which receipts could be invested, boosting annual
revenue by a huge amount.

Soon the female treasurer put a stop to the long-standing practice of investing largely in bank certificates of deposit, turning to
U.S. government securities and New York banks. Richards estimates that the result of these and other practices designed "to
bring the Texas treasury into the twentieth century" pumped
four billion dollars more into the state's coffers than the system
she inherited would have produced during her tenure.

Although many voters considered fiscal reform to be her
most dramatic achievement, another remarkable transition
took place. During Richards's two terms of office, the number
of women employees rose from 35 percent of the staff to 65 percent. The number of African Americans increased to 14 percent

Ann Richards catapulted onto the national stage when she delivered the keynote address at the 1988 Democratic Convention.

ARCHIVES & INFORMATION SERVICES DIVISION, TEXAS STATE LIBRARY

and Hispanics to 27 percent—levels that she estimates to be close to the profile of citizens in the state.

It is not surprising that her many admirers urged Richards to seek the governorship in 1988. Criticized as "a liberal under the influence of the eastern establishment," she fought a hard but successful campaign, delivering one dynamic speech after another. Afterward, television networks sent crews to Austin to show the nation "this new breed of politician."

From the governor's mansion Richards announced that she would do everything possible to guarantee that in the future "schoolchildren of the state can open their history books and find in them pictures of people who look like them." Warmly praised by many—locally, nationally, and internationally— the Democrat was despised by voters who did not like her "ultraliberal point of view."

When Richards ran for reelection in 1994, Republicans chose as her opponent George W. Bush, the eldest son of "the man born with a silver foot in his mouth." To the surprise of many, nearly half of the women who voted in the election backed

Bush. According to Texas journalist Molly Ivins, this reaction reflected the fact that more than half of all Texans disapproved of President Bill Clinton. Whether or not that is a valid analysis of her loss, her bid for another term was backed by two million voters.

Regardless of what projects she plans for the future, Richards can take pride in her accomplishments. Her friends happily predict, "Ann may be out for now, but she's far from down!"

7

Texas City

Deadly Prelude

On the morning of April 16, 1947, a panicked call went to the bridge of the ocean liner *Grandcamp*, docked at Texas City.

"Longshoremen smell smoke! They think it's coming out of the number four hold!"

Capt. Charles de Guillebon nodded but did not look up from his desk. "Send somebody down to find the fire and pour some water on it," he ordered. "Sounds like a cigarette was dropped in the trash."

Nearly filled with hundred-pound bags of fertilizer, hold number four meant hope to thousands of French farmers. Their country had been devastated by World War II and was gradually recovering. Under the Marshall Plan, the United States was sending several commodities to speed up that recovery. The free fertilizer would be a great help.

By the time three or four men began to move the cargo in search of the blaze, smoke had increased in volume and was darker. When half a dozen fertilizer bags were discovered with holes blackened around the edges from fire, water was poured on each of them. One member of the crew who spoke no English grumbled, "We are ruining the hopes of at least one farmer."

Back on deck a firefighter was surprised when black smoke streaked with bright orange suddenly billowed from the hold. Someone on the dock decided that the Texas City volunteer fire department might be needed, so he called to request a tank truck.

When the volunteer firemen arrived, de Guillebon assured them that everything was under control. Pointing to the hold

46

in question, he explained that he had closed the hatch and thrown a wet tarpaulin over it. Just to be on the safe side, he explained, he was in the process of pumping steam into the hold.

"That ship could still blow," fire chief Harry Baumgartner pointed out. In the local newspaper he had seen a partial list of what the French ocean liner expected to take across the Atlantic: more than sixty thousand bales of farm products—binder twine, cotton, and tobacco—agricultural and well-drilling equipment, shelled peanuts, fertilizer, and a dozen or more cases of ammunition for handguns.

If a single shotgun shell or pistol cartridge should become heated to the point of explosion, "It could cause all hell to break loose," said Baumgartner. When questioned, he explained, "A few cases of ammo wouldn't do much damage by themselves, but they could set off all that artificial guano."

Alone and properly handled, the active ingredient in man-made fertilizer poses no danger. If dampened with fuel oil, it becomes a powerful explosive. Just how deadly those sacks of fertilizer could be, the residents of the port learned that morning.

Cautious firemen urged that the *Grandcamp* should be towed from the pier into Galveston Bay, and preparations for the move got under way just before 9:00 A.M. This work was cut short when more than two thousand tons of fire-heated fertilizer exploded in the number four hold. A single tremendous blast blew the *Grandcamp* to bits.

In Denver, Colorado, earthquake scientists watched their seismographic needles jiggle. Was it possible, they wondered, that California was in the throes of its worst-ever earthquake?

Military experts who specialized in explosives later estimated that the Texas City blast unleashed energy equivalent to that of 250 blockbuster bombs of World War II. To make matters worse for the port on Galveston Bay, the epicenter of the explosion was below ground level. That meant it did more physical damage than the midair detonation of the first atomic bomb at Hiroshima.

A death toll that everyone accepted as accurate was never reached. According to the most authoritative analyses, at least 550 persons died in the blast and in some of the many buildings that were leveled or set on fire. That total does not include

The site of the explosion in Texas City, looking west, shows the damage to the Monsanto plant and the other port facilities.

missing persons or the twenty-five hundred to three thousand people who were injured or left homeless.

De Guillebon and most members of his crew were simply lost in the explosion. Baumgartner and some of his firefighters suffered the same fate; so did longshoremen and men lounging about the pier.

Four vessels lying not far from the *Grandcamp* felt the full force of the blast that cut one of them, the *Wilson B. Keene*, in two. A segment of the ship that measured more than 250 feet in length was tossed on top of a warehouse that collapsed under its weight. Aboard the *High Flyer*, the wind created by the explosion was many times that of the worst hurricane ever experienced in Gulf waters. Flames from the ship's boiler room may have been forced into the hold during this blast of wind. It was impossible to tow the vessel out to sea. Also loaded with an unknown quantity of ammonium nitrate, the *High Flyer* exploded a few hours later.

Monsanto Chemical Company, with about five hundred employees and an additional one hundred construction workers on the job, suffered some of the most costly damage on

The cargo ship Wilson B. Keene *was blown in half by the explosion. It had been docked near the* Grandchamp *and the* High Flyer.

land. Nearly one-third of the work force died, and others were injured, many by the collapse of a building that had been rated as capable of withstanding anything nature might throw at it.

Every structure on the waterfront was leveled, oil refineries caught fire, and the downtown business district looked as though it had been bombed. Even small residences situated a distance from the pier did not escape unscathed. According to newspaper accounts, "No pane of glass in Texas City was left unshattered."

Mayor J. Curtis Trahan activated Civilian Defense teams and launched the work of caring for the injured. As news of the disaster spread, help was rushed to the stricken city by the American Red Cross, the U.S. Army Corps of Engineers, firefighting companies from every nearby city, the Texas Rangers, the Salvation Army, and numerous other organizations. By afternoon, an ambulance with a medical team from Dallas—nearly 250 miles away—was on the scene.

Under the direction of Trahan, the gruesome work of recovering bodies began. Before the job was finished, the high school gymnasium was crowded with about two hundred blanket-covered victims. More than half of those who died were never found.

Measured by any standard, this explosion constituted the worst industrial disaster the nation had ever suffered. Half a century later, that record still stands. At least twenty-five hundred lawsuits were filed by more than three times that number of plaintiffs. Since the fertilizer came from factories operating under U.S. government contracts and army officials had clearly specified the danger involved in handling ammonium nitrate, suits directed against the government and its agencies were not allowed. In 1953 Congress, however, approved a payment of sixteen million dollars to the survivors in the city of sixteen thousand residents.

As a result of the disaster, the U.S. Coast Guard set new guidelines. Any person or corporation loading or unloading five hundred or more pounds of ammonium nitrate was required to obtain a permit, and the handler was required to work with the potential explosive at a location remote from daily traffic by numerous persons.

These controls have seemingly succeeded in limiting this kind of industrial calamity. The bombing of the Alfred P. Murrah Federal Building in Oklahoma City in April 1995, however, cruelly reminded the nation of the explosive potential of common fertilizer. Had the diabolic act not been related to domestic terrorism, the country could have seen the Texas City disaster as a prelude to Oklahoma City.

Part 2
Off the Beaten Path

Lady Bird Johnson was keenly interested in the KTBC radio station's equipment and its condition, as well as its balance sheet.

8

Lady Bird

Percentage Points

Records of the Marshall, Texas, High School reveal that in 1927 three girls were the leading candidates for class valedictorian. One of them, Claudia Alta Taylor, known as Lady Bird, did not want the top spot.

Explaining her unwillingness to graduate as top scholar, she later said that she'd "just as soon have the smallpox" as offer the customary valedictory speech. Keeping a close eye on the other two contenders, the fifteen-year-old may have deliberately shaved her test scores to give her a grade point average of 94. Thus Maurine Cranson became salutatorian, with 94.5, and Emma Boehringer's 95 allowed her to make the valedictory at graduation.

Born in Karnack, Lady Bird was just five years old when her mother died after tripping over a collie and falling down a long flight of steps. Reared by an aunt who came to look after her, at age thirteen Lady Bird persuaded her father to teach her to drive. She needed that skill, she pointed out, to make the twenty-eight-mile round trip to the Marshall High School in the county seat.

After succeeding in her scheme to avoid the valedictory speech, Lady Bird enrolled in the University of Texas at Austin. She planned to take a four-year course of study to become certified as a second-grade teacher. Upon graduation in 1933, though, she decided to remain another year to get a degree in journalism—a field in which she had always been interested.

With two bachelor's degrees in hand, Lady Bird began to look for a job. "I wanted to go to some faraway romantic spot like Hawaii or Alaska," she recalled afterward. "I might have gone to one of them, had not the secretary of Congressman Richard Kleburg suddenly entered my life with a bang." Asked to characterize twenty-six-year-old Lyndon Baines Johnson, Jesse Kellam of Austin's KTBC television station said, "He drove himself, and either drove or led those who worked with him and for him at a hard clip."

In 1934 Lady Bird and Lyndon's wedding in San Antonio pushed all notions of "some faraway romantic spot" from her mind. Her husband had then become state director of the National Youth Administration, and she became concerned with young adults desperately in need of jobs.

Life took another turn in 1937, when LBJ chose to run for a seat in the U.S. House of Representatives. He had a following, but he lacked the money to finance a political campaign. Lady Bird persuaded her father to advance Lyndon ten thousand dollars against her inheritance. From the day her husband was seated as a congressman, Lady Bird was a full-time Washington wife.

"It was fortunate that Lyndon and I had one common trait— thrift," she recalled of her early years in the nation's capital. "His salary was just $267 a month and rent, alone, cost us $42.50. Somehow, we managed to buy a government bond every month, thinking that the $18.75 we put into it would someday help us to raise children." Reared in economic comfort, Lady Bird knew that she would someday come into money from her mother's estate, but in 1937 her inheritance was too far off to affect their spartan lifestyle.

Five years later Lady Bird's share of her mother's estate came to her, and she was faced with another dilemma. What to do with that much money?

Friends told her that the owners of a small radio station in Austin were anxious to sell it and would probably do so at a rock-bottom price. Both she and Lyndon had dreamed of owning and publishing a newspaper, but they knew they couldn't afford it. Perhaps the radio station would satisfy their urge.

Potential problems loomed, however. The three partners who had launched the station in 1937 were disappointed to find that they had little return on their initial investment of $27,000. Five years after going on the air, the station's debts

Though she was always amiable, staffers were unanimous in saying that "Lady Bird ran a tight ship."

amounted to nearly $20,000. When the partners chose to sell the station in 1940 for $32,000, they found no buyers. Handicapping the sale was the fact that the station was licensed to operate only during the daylight hours, it had no network affiliation, and other radio stations virtually crowded it off the air.

Lady Bird's inheritance included several thousand acres of land in Alabama, but her cash assets amounted to $21,000. She and Lyndon consulted with a radio veteran, reviewing the pros and cons of the purchase for the better part of a day. As midnight neared, Lady Bird said, "If we are going to go into it, let's do it right. It may take everything we have, but it's a gamble I want to make."

The Johnsons purchased the radio station, and Lady Bird plunged herself into the day-to-day operations as soon as the purchase was final. She remained on the job for seven months and made only occasional brief trips to Washington. According to insider Jesse Kellam, when a major decision had to be made, "Mrs. Johnson always had the final word."

Lyndon B. Johnson, though not a great communicator like Ronald Reagan, quickly became at ease when dealing with the new mass media.

Advertising revenues failed to meet operating expenses. So Lady Bird received permission to increase her listening area. She cut costs wherever possible and personally supervised the advertising accounts. Finally, in August 1943 KTBC showed a monthly profit of $18 and never looked back in debt.

Ten years later the Federal Communications Commission made television channels available. The Johnsons pondered moving into the new medium. Texas then had four television stations, all of which alleged to be losing money. Lady Bird consulted with Leonard Marks, general counsel of the FCC during World War II who later served as director of the U.S. Information Agency. Marks knew television about as well as anyone in the nation, and he was able to point out both the risks and the opportunities of expanding into this field.

The senator's wife did not waver. She applied for a VHF license at a time when most investors were interested in UHF television. She learned that few receiving sets were capable of receiving UHF broadcasts, which meant that her decision to pursue the VHF route was right, and it took only a few years to show how very right she was.

In 1963, when Vice President Lyndon Johnson succeeded to the presidency, Lady Bird resigned as chairman of KTBC's board and placed her holdings in a trusteeship. KTBC was estimated to be worth close to seven million dollars. Its signal reached dozens of counties, in many of which it had little or no competition.

Lady Bird had numerous opportunities to sell the station at a huge profit, but she resisted until 1987, when she accepted $27,500,000—a capital gain of 110,000 percent on her original risky investment. No other Texas businesswoman and few businessmen have matched that accomplishment.

9
Galveston

Curse Reversed

Jean Laffite, the legendary gentleman pirate, called his men together some time in 1820. They had just won a bloody victory over the Karankawas Indians—natives of Gálvez Island on which Laffite had established a base. Thus the tiny pirate village of Campeachy was no longer threatened by the warriors who had preyed earlier on the pirates.

"We have put down the Karankawas," Laffite is said to have told his men. "It was a mistake to come here. We must find another hideaway. This little island is under a curse, for it is named after a Spaniard."

Spanish surveyors had named the island in 1785 for Count Bernardo de Gálvez, viceroy of Mexico. Interestingly, the viceroy was said to have schemed to establish an independent Mexico, and he once boasted that he had rid the Gulf of Mexico of pirates. Laffite and his cutthroats had now come to the area, but the viceroy's name was anathema to the French-born adventurer.

Laffite and his men were soon dislodged from the area when a U.S. expedition was dispatched to destroy the pirate colony. The pirates torched Campeachy and shook the dust of Gálvez Island from their shoes. Meanwhile, Mexican authorities saw the island's potential as a great port, but their settlement was overrun during the Texas Revolution and served as the base of naval operations against Mexico for the Republic of Texas and was made the temporary capital in 1836.

After Sam Houston's tiny Texas army defeated the Mexican army under Gen. Antonio López de Santa Anna in the battle

Jean Laffite, whose base was on the island for a period, sent Andrew Jackson seven thousand musket flints before the battle of New Orleans.

of San Jacinto, a few Americans made Gálvez Island their permanent home. Soon they began calling its already bustling port Galveston.

The slender island from which goods flowed to and from Atlantic Coast ports, Great Britain, and Europe was only twenty-eight miles long. Hence, by 1900 longtime residents were beginning to grumble that the island was too crowded and too congested. That year the census revealed that Galveston, whose population was approaching forty thousand, was fourth in size among the cities of the Lone Star State.

Some people were concerned that most of the island lay at sea level or slightly below. The elevation of its highest ridge was not quite nine feet, which was hardly sufficient protection should a hurricane threaten the island.

The owners of the elegant five-story Tremont Hotel scoffed at the mention of hurricanes. Comdr. Matthew Fontaine Maury, known as the father of oceanography, had taken a keen interest in Galveston, they pointed out. After completing an

As governor of Spanish Louisiana, Bernardo de Gálvez had jurisdiction over the island that was named Galveston in his honor.

DICTIONARY OF AMERICAN PORTRAITS

elaborate survey, Maury had announced that no tropical storm coming from the West Indies would come anywhere near Galveston. In a subsequent writing, he asserted that the destruction of Galveston by a tropical storm was not in the realm of possibility.

If there were any danger from tropical storms, Galveston's civic leaders conceded, their "Queen City" would not have attracted so much wealth. Investors had erected an opera house, a trio of concert halls, and twenty hotels. The owners of these and other establishments were confident that nearly fifty steamship offices and at least sixty industries would bring them sufficient business.

In that verdict they were correct, but their faith in Maury's optimism proved disastrous. Before sunset on Friday, September 7, 1900, a red-and-black flag flapped frantically above the beach that a few hours earlier had been crowded with tourists. Isaac Cline, local head of the U.S. Weather Bureau, had reason to believe that a storm of some magnitude was headed toward the city from the West Indies. Cline's information was both

Internationally renowned oceanographer Matthew Maury was convinced that Galveston residents need have no fear of hurricanes.

vague and spotty. In 1900 meteorologists could not locate storms at sea or follow their paths.

Before daylight on Saturday, September 8, heavy surf strengthened the bureau chief's apprehension. Although warned of the possible danger, thrill seekers braved light rain and crowded the beaches to see the monstrous breakers rolling angrily shoreward.

By noon seawater had moved into the lower sections of the island, forcing one-eighth of the island's residents to evacuate their homes and businesses and seek refuge on higher ground. Within two or three hours after the exodus began, half of the city was under water.

At the weather bureau, Cline saw his high-wind gauge register more than eighty miles per hour before the instrument was blown away around 5:00 P.M. Shortly afterward, the full fury of the hurricane descended on Galveston.

Cline retreated to his home, which stood on relatively high ground nearly a half mile from the ocean. Since it was reputed to have been built to withstand wind and water, the home was soon crowded with Cline's neighbors. No accurate count was ever published after the hurricane, but it was estimated that at least thirty-six people died in the residence, thus it may have been a refuge for fifty or more.

The citizens of Galveston were proud of their splendid city hall, and many of them hurried toward it when the water began to rise. Others crowded into many of the island's forty churches. In the heart of the business district, the impressive Tremont Hotel opened its doors to an estimated eight hundred to a thousand refugees. As the water began to fill the hotel lobby, the people scurried for the mezzanine and higher floors.

The howling winds reached greater intensity, and tiles were torn from the roofs of mansions—some hurled through the air with such velocity that they decapitated people unfortunate to be without shelter. Though severely damaged, most of the elegant residences rode out the storm, but not so the homes of ordinary folk and the shanties of longshoremen and industrial plant workers.

Pounded by the surf on the Gulf side and slowly slipping under the storm tide from the harbor, by 4 P.M. the entire island was inundated. Frame houses were wrenched from their foundations to float and capsize in the surf and then batter the buildings still standing. The wind reached 96 miles per hour at 5:15, just before the anemometer blew away. The highest wind velocity was estimated at 120 miles per hour.

Suddenly the wind shifted from east to southeast, sending a five-foot wave across the city. It was the moment of greatest destruction. Brick walls began to give way in some buildings where many had sought shelter. Sections of streetcar track swept through the streets, leveling everything they contacted. Hundreds died within moments, but ironically the wind shift saved the lives of hundreds more who were clinging to their homes and would have been swept out to sea.

When the winds began to subside, rescuers took to the streets with lanterns. They found bodies by the dozen, by the score, and by the hundred. Eventually it was established that at least six thousand had lost their lives in one of the most deadly natural disasters in U.S. history. There were far too many corpses to be handled in conventional ways.

According to a widely circulated estimate, damage in Galveston (above) from 120-mile-per-hour winds ran to fifteen million dollars.

On Monday, September 10, an estimated seven hundred bodies were piled upon a barge that was towed to sea to be dumped. When large numbers of the dead washed ashore Tuesday morning, attempts at burial at sea were abandoned. Hundreds of bodies were consigned to hastily dug trenches; hundreds of others were cremated on immense funeral pyres fueled by the lumber from destroyed buildings.

The spirit of the people of Galveston refused to be broken by the death and destruction hurled upon them by the hurricane. Seventy-eight-year-old Clara Barton, founder of the American Red Cross, arrived to contribute to the relief work—her last public appearance in that capacity. When the *Galveston News* resumed publication in its half-destroyed building, bold headlines assured readers, "Galveston Shall Rise Again!"

Corps engineer Bill Jakeway inspects Galveston's present seawall.

Regarded by the editors as more assurance than prediction, that headline was quickly followed by massive efforts to prevent another disaster from the sea. Under the direction of Brig. Gen. Henry M. Robert, the U.S. Army Corps of Engineers constructed a massive three-mile-long seawall, which was later extended to ten miles in length.

As a further precaution, in case evacuation should become necessary in the future, the island was linked with the mainland by a wide and sturdy causeway. Using fill dirt and oyster shells, the grade of the whole city was elevated. Some points that had previously been below sea level were raised as much as fifteen feet.

Today the Galveston District of the U.S. Army Corps of Engineers is responsible for the entire Texas coastline—from Louisiana to Mexico. With an annual budget in the range of one hundred million dollars, the district supervises navigation, flood control, and protection from hurricanes and floods.

Immense jetties—the world's longest at nearly thirty-six thousand feet—now project into the Gulf of Mexico and make the Galveston Channel navigable by large ships. If all the goods that pass through the Galveston District in a year were loaded on barges, the line of loaded barges would stretch from Galveston to Shanghai.

Many environmentalists know that the Galveston District is the winter home of the rare and endangered whooping crane. Less familiar is the fact that the Gulf Intracoastal Waterway, of which Galveston is a key component, provides Texans with 145,000 jobs and annually generates twenty billion dollars in industrial activity.

Galveston's early nickname of "Queen City," almost forgotten in the aftermath of the hurricane of 1900, is today singularly appropriate. Not only is the Galveston District far safer than many ports that have never experienced disaster, it is the Lone Star State's queen city of chemical production and shipping.

As an afterword, the Galveston hurricane of 1900 also affected lives throughout the country in an unusual way. The city's weak mayoral government could not deal effectively with the disaster. As a result, the state legislature provided for a city government charter to opt for a five-member city commission. The plan was such a success that by 1917 about five hundred cities had adopted the commission form of government. In 1961 Galveston changed its form of city government again, this time to a city manager system.

10
Zachary Taylor
A Second Career

James K. Polk, supported by Andrew Jackson to succeed John Tyler as president of the United States, made Texas his biggest campaign issue. Many of his followers waved special flags that showed his portrait inside a circle of twenty-six white stars—one for each state. To the right of this emblem, on a red-and-white striped field, was a single large blue star that symbolized Texas.

This ambition of the relatively unknown politician from Tennessee was thwarted, however, by Tyler. In the interim between Polk's election and the inauguration, Tyler recommended that Texas be admitted by a joint congressional resolution, which did not require a two-thirds vote. Northern leaders had obstructed earlier efforts to add Texas to the union because the new state would be a slave state. Tyler's action was constitutionally questionable, but it succeeded, and he signed the resolution two days before leaving office. Mexico, of course, refused to accept the annexation of its former province and disputed the boundary of the new state, which it contended was the Nueces River rather than the Rio Grande.

The acquisition of California from Mexico was another of Polk's goals. Accordingly, he dispatched a representative to Mexico City to settle claims between Americans and Mexico in return for recognition of the Rio Grande as the southern border of Texas, to offer five million dollars for the area known as New Mexico, and to negotiate the purchase of California. The Mexican government, however, was not interested in these proposals and refused to see the American representative.

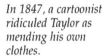

In 1847, a cartoonist ridiculed Taylor as mending his own clothes.

SIMPLICITY OF OLD ZACK'S HABITS.

Polk was delighted. He sent troops into the disputed region of Texas with orders to "defend the Rio Grande." Because the president despised Winfield Scott, commanding general of the U.S. Army, Polk ordered the less colorful Brig. Gen. Zachary Taylor to command this force and to occupy and patrol the contested land.

Taylor, a sixty-one-year-old professional soldier who seldom wore any insignia of rank, even on those rare occasions when he donned a uniform, was pleased but surprised. He knew quite well that his three thousand men would be challenging a proud nation with a long history and a huge army. Should war break out, it would involve the United States in its first conflict on foreign soil.

Taylor's troops reached their destination on the Rio Grande on March 28, 1846, directly across from a Mexican city. Since the river was only about one hundred yards wide, Lt. U. S. Grant casually remarked, "It would be tolerably easy to throw a few balls into the heart of Matamoros." Taylor, however, directed his men to erect a stout fortress and mount their heaviest guns on its ramparts. While their fifteen-foot-thick earthen walls were being completed, a Mexican force crossed the river at another point and clashed with the Americans on April 25. President Polk seized this opportunity to charge on May 11 that the enemy had "passed the boundary of the United States, invaded our territory, and shed American blood upon American soil." With the presidential message still resounding, Congress declared war on Mexico two days later. In doing so, they knew that they would alienate large numbers of Americans who felt the war was morally wrong.

While the opposing forces faced one another across the Rio Grande, an estimated 7 percent of Taylor's men deserted. Meanwhile, reinforcements bolstered Mexican strength to about five thousand men. Taylor's army was no more than twenty-five hundred strong. Knowing that he was outnumbered, the American general decided to leave five hundred men to hold the fort and see if he could outflank the enemy with the rest.

A fierce exchange of cannon fire began on May 3 and lasted for five days between Matamoros and Taylor's fort. Meanwhile, the American general defeated a Mexican force at Palo Alto on May 8 and another at Resaca de la Palmas on May 9. The Mexicans fell back, and Taylor's army seized Matamoros on May 15.

Taylor occupied Monterey after a five-day battle that was concluded by a generous armistice that allowed the Mexican force to withdraw with its weapons and stipulated a two-month cessation of hostilities. When news of the terms reached Washington, the president furiously dashed off a terse order directing Taylor to resume the offensive immediately. At the same time, Polk noted that his general in the field was receiving very good reviews in the newspapers, and Taylor was a member of the opposition party. Thus the president elevated Winfield Scott to supreme command in Mexico and diverted some of Taylor's troops to Scott's army.

Further complicating the situation in Mexico, the former Mexican president, Gen. Antonio López de Santa Anna, who had been in exile in Cuba, now returned to Mexico City and assumed the presidency again. Santa Anna then gathered a large force to confront Taylor and attacked Taylor's army at

N CURRIER LITHOGRAPH, LIBRARY OF CONGRESS

Battle of Buena Vista, with Taylor brandishing saber to give directions (on white horse, right).

Buena Vista on February 23, 1847. Although Taylor suffered heavy casualties, his army inflicted three times as many casualties upon the Mexicans. Taylor, twice hit but not seriously wounded during the melee, became an instant hero as soon as word of his exploit reached the United States. A correspondent for a Philadelphia newspaper confided to readers that "The general may be out of command, due to the ill will of the president, but he is far from being down."

The final campaign of the war began with the landing of Scott's army at Veracruz in March. Scott then began the drive to Mexico City by defeating Santa Anna at Cerro Gordo in April, winning battles at Contreras and Churubusco in August, and storming Casa Mata, Molino del Rey, and Chapultepec in September before occupying Mexico City on September 14.

The war was concluded by the treaty of Guadalupe Hidalgo, under whose terms the U.S. agreed to pay fifteen million dollars for the largest annexation of land since the 1803 Louisiana Purchase. Stipulating that the Rio Grande was the southern border of Texas, Mexico ceded to the United States land from which the future states of California, Nevada, Utah, Wyoming, Colorado, New Mexico, and Arizona were carved.

Four months after the ratification of the treaty, the Whig Party convened its national convention in Philadelphia. Many delegates were pledged to Henry Clay, Winfield Scott, and Daniel Webster. In spite of this formidable field of famous opponents, Zachary Taylor won the nomination on the fourth ballot.

In November Taylor faced Democrat Lewis Cass of Michigan and former president Martin Van Buren, who had been nominated by the Free Soil Party. The third-party element fractured the traditional Democratic vote and sent Taylor to the Executive Mansion.

In thanking his supporters when his electoral victory was announced, the voice of the hero of Monterey became a bit husky. "I owe everything to Texas," Taylor said. "Had there been no boundary dispute with Mexico, I would have ended my career in some wretched military post far on the western frontier."

11
O. Henry

Spare Time

Although O. Henry's short stories are largely set in and around New York, filled with the color and spirit of turn-of-the-century America, his early adult life was spent in Texas. Perhaps the most influential moment of his life occurred there as well. After sixteen years in residence, he left the Lone Star State, but not exactly on his own terms.

Born and reared in Greensboro, North Carolina, O. Henry's real name was William Sydney Porter. He had a brilliant mind and a fertile imagination and amazed his teachers by solving mathematical problems with his right hand while he sketched with his left. He attended no school except one that his aunt taught. His cartoons won him a scholarship to a North Carolina college, but he lacked the funds to pay for his books and supplies. Thus at the age of fifteen he turned his back on the classroom and never came back. Since his mother had died of tuberculosis in 1865 and his father wasted most of his time fooling around with ideas for a perpetual motion machine, the boy explained, somebody in the family had to work for a living.

Will found a job in his uncle's little corner drugstore. An apprentice pharmacist, he stuck to his uncle's drugstore for five years and might have stayed in Greensboro for the rest of his life had he had not come across a thrilling article in one of the many magazines he borrowed from the rack.

According to a fellow who had been there, Texas was the place to be. It was described as "growing faster than the sideburns of a thirty-year old" and as having so many jobs that all

During his boyhood,
O. Henry spent much of his
spare time at the home of
his grandparents.

a person had to do was to pick out one that suited him and go to work.

Nearly every paragraph of that early travel article seemed to strike mental sparks as Will Porter raced excitedly through it. Since he knew some folk who had gone there from North Carolina earlier, he was sure he could find work on their ranch. Besides, Texas air would probably help him get rid of a persistent cough that made strangers sometimes think he might be in the early stages of tuberculosis. One evening, he surprised his uncle and aunt by announcing his plans of going to Texas and working on a ranch.

Ranch life in LaSalle County, which he pursued for a couple of years, did not prove quite as idyllic as he had imagined it to be from a distance. He hated to get up before the sun to feed the cattle, and he had to ride a bony old horse to get to the nearest village, which did not even have a drugstore.

There is little argument that his time on the ranch served as his education. He carried a dictionary with him regularly, he read the family's well-stocked library, and he wrote stories, frequently tearing them up when he failed to please himself.

Porter (seated, left, 1886) briefly made regular appearances with what he and his colleagues called "The Hill City Quartette."

After two years, his friends sold their ranch, and Will moved on to the sprawling town of Austin—population, ten thousand. He was disappointed to find that the Texas capital was smaller than Greensboro, but he liked the looks of the place— especially the campus of the University of Texas.

In Austin he tended to waste his days working in a cigar store and a real estate office. He wrote some friends in Greensboro that the vast acreages of public land offered him a great deal of job security. He toyed with learning to play the guitar. At night, however, he toured the town, saloon by saloon. Will

For a period, Porter was one of eleven full-time employees of the Texas State Land Office.

Porter had a prodigious capacity for alcohol, and he was sociable while drunk. He would spin tales for anyone who would listen and join in on any revelry that could be devised within a bar. He caroused in Austin for twelve years. He even married, but eloped with his wife because that made the affair more adventurous.

Marriage failed to keep Will Porter home though. In time, he began to feel as if he were caged. Athol, his wife, was a frail woman suffering with tuberculosis, and she became even more frail after giving birth to their daughter, Margaret, in 1889. Porter was able to sell some of his stories occasionally, but the income was slight.

Always a smooth talker whose friends said he could sell butter and eggs to any farm woman who would open her door to him, he found a job as teller in the First National Bank. Banking practices were very lax and audits very few. Porter once spent two days trying to find a hundred dollar shortage from his till before a bank officer confessed that he had "borrowed" it and forgotten to write an IOU.

Will Porter's heart was never in his teller's cage. He still wrote humorous stories about everyday life and sketched the faces of the bank's customers. In the evening he worked on his own weekly paper, the *Rolling Stone*. His cartoons and satires sold well at first, and then the paper began to lose advertisers. Almost always at a loss for cash, he even tried digging for lost treasure in a nearby canyon.

In 1894 a bank examiner found a serious shortage in Porter's till. He was accused of embezzlement. Despite the pleas of his co-workers, the bank refused to drop the charges, and Porter resigned. His father-in-law negotiated a settlement, compensating the bank with fifteen hundred dollars of his own money, and the grand jury cleared the former bank clerk of the charges.

An editor of the *Houston Daily Post* had been reviewing Porter's writings and liked them enough to give Will an assignment. His daily newspaper column, initially called "Tales of the Town," gradually changed its character and became "Some Postscripts." While there was nothing particularly charming about his new position, Porter might have stayed at the *Daily Post* and gradually shaped his writing skill had other matters not developed in Austin.

Federal investigators found the books of the First National Bank filled with irregularities. The bank's officers knew they had a scapegoat, and in 1896 they swore out a warrant requiring Porter to stand trial on charges of embezzling $4,702.94.

Pure panic set in when damning legal papers arrived from Austin. Porter knew so little about bookkeeping that he easily could have made some mistakes that might lead investigators to decide that he really was a thief. Facing the possibility of a trial and knowing he could not afford to hire a lawyer, Porter decided to flee. Taking the train from Houston to Austin, he switched trains about fifty miles down the track and headed for New Orleans, where he booked passage on a steamer to Honduras.

The island nation did not have an extradition treaty with the United States, so Porter was safe from the Texas Rangers or any other lawmen of his adopted state. He spent three months in Honduras doing little else but drinking and living off the generosity of a fugitive train robber whom he befriended. He wrote home to ask his wife to join him, but he learned instead that she was gravely ill. Under the circumstances, the accused man felt that there was nothing he could do but go to her side and try to comfort her in her last hours.

Athol Estes Porter did not get much comfort when her husband arrived in Austin. A deputy sheriff soon had Porter in handcuffs. After arranging bail, Porter seemed numb. He sold one of his stories to a national magazine, his first major sale, and the editors wanted other stories, but Athol and the aunt who had raised him both died within a short time. He had a daughter to raise, and his character was on trial.

When the bank officials accused Porter of stealing at least two checks, the former teller refused to offer a defense. The charges of pocketing the large amounts were dropped, but he was convicted of stealing $299.60. No one has yet to agree on his guilt or innocence. Some say he took the punishment for someone else, others that he was a rascal and easily a crook. He was sentenced to five years in the federal penitentiary at Columbus, Ohio.

Almost as soon as he was behind bars, the drifter who had tried his hand at several jobs and succeeded in none was assigned to the prison pharmacy. Since the demands made on him were slight, he had a great deal of time to devote to writing. Several of the stories he penned in prison were published, so when he was released he went to New York and found a job as an assistant editor of a magazine. For reasons unknown, he preferred to write under pseudonyms and tried several before he settled upon O. Henry.

During the first two decades of this century, the Texan by choice who left the state wearing handcuffs was the most widely read author of short stories. By 1910, many of them had been collected in a series of nine successful books. After his death that year, four more volumes of his short stories were published.

No other American writer who specialized in short stories has produced so vast a volume of material in such a short time. Even when he wrote about New York City subjects, his experiences on the ranch plus Austin and Houston provided him with both characters and details. Crushed in spirit by his conviction on charges that today might not stand up in court, endless hours of free time in an Ohio prison turned a Texas drifter into a best-selling author.

Part 3
Westward Ho!

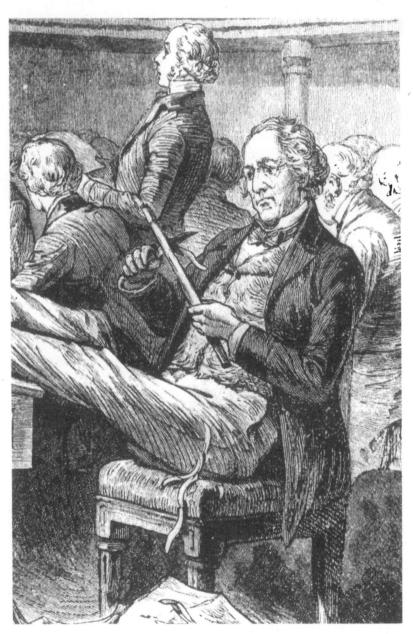

Describing his term as a congressman, Houston said, "It was so boring I could spit."

12

Sam Houston

From Wayward Son to Revolutionary Father

Fourteen is a troublesome age," sighed the Widow Houston, who had moved to Tennessee from Virginia. "Sam gives me as much trouble as his five brothers and three sisters put together. School ain't for the likes of him; he didn't stay with his books for even one year. Guess I won't be surprised at anything he does."

Not long after that verdict was expressed, Sam turned his back on his family and wandered into one of the fifty or so villages of the Cherokees. He had no trouble winning acceptance and soon learned the Kituhwa dialect that was used by his new family.

Tall and strong, by the time he was sixteen Sam looked as though he had never worn anything except a deerskin breechcloth. In a rare gesture, Chief Oo-loo-te-ka formally adopted the adolescent white as his son and gave him an Indian name that meant "the Raven." As a gesture of appreciation, the youth went on a shopping spree in nearby Maryville, where he bought about one hundred dollars' worth of gifts for the Cherokees—on credit.

After nearly three years as an adopted Cherokee, Sam suddenly returned to the society of his parents. When acquaintances asked him what he had been doing during his three years among the Cherokees, he bragged that he had spent most of the time "making love and reading Homer's *Iliad*."

In spite of his very limited education, Sam decided that the only way he could support himself was to open a school. His months as a schoolmaster came to an abrupt end when he enlisted to fight the British and their Indian allies in what came to be known as the War of 1812.

His commander, Andrew Jackson, was impressed with him and soon made the Tennessee youth his protégé, promoting him to the rank of ensign. Having marched to Alabama, Sam was in the forefront of fighting at the battle of Horseshoe Bend. There Jackson's soldiers won a decisive victory at the cost of numerous casualties. One of them was Sam, who took two bullets and an arrow that pierced his intestines. The wound never healed, and for the rest of his life he had to change bandages regularly.

After having read law for a short time, the Virginia native was elected attorney general for the Nashville district in 1819. Two years later, through the influence of Jackson, he was made a major general and put in command of the Tennessee militia.

Jackson's protégé went to Washington as a member of the House of Representatives in 1823. Some members of society snubbed the backwoodsman and said that he was a Cherokee who had no place in the capital. He responded by whittling on the floor of Congress and defending this practice by describing sessions of the body as "so boring that I could spit."

He may have been impatient with the tedium of political office, but that did not prevent his seeking and winning the governorship of Tennessee in 1827. Measured by any standard, at age thirty-four the self-educated soldier-statesman had arrived.

Soon Governor Houston found himself attracted to young Eliza Allen "as though drawn by a magnet." They were married in her father's Cumberland River mansion on January 22, 1829. At the ceremony the groom was described as being "the figure of elegance in a suit of black velvet, topped by a Spanish cloak lined with scarlet satin."

The newlyweds took up residence in Nashville, and Houston prepared to open his campaign for reelection. Suddenly, on April 9, less than twelve weeks after their wedding, nineteen-year-old Eliza went home to her father. A few days later the governor followed his wife to the Allen mansion, where a mutual friend later said, "Husband and wife parted forever. What passed no one knows, as the lips of both were ever afterward sealed."

Houston's only written record of the separation is in the form of a letter he wrote to his father-in-law. In it, he praised Eliza's virtue and swore that he loved her before adding: "She was cold to me, & I thought did not love me. She owns that such was one cause of my unhappiness. You can judge how unhappy I was to think I was united to a woman that did not love me." Eliza waited seven years to file for divorce, which she obtained on the grounds of abandonment.

Although it was Eliza who returned home, it was her bridegroom who soon became a runaway. Houston resigned as governor on April 29, not quite three weeks after the breakup of his marriage.

One of his cousins, Emily Drennen, told friends, "He wouldn't say a word about the separation under any circumstances." In later years, many people tried to pry an explanation from him of why his marriage failed. No one ever heard the story; he always closed his eyes briefly, shook his head, and turned the conversation to another topic.

Thomas Boyers, a resident of Austin, Texas, who earlier lived in Gallatin, Tennessee, knew both Sam and Eliza intimately. Years after their mysterious separation, he described the Houston he knew as "always the cavalier, booted and spurred, 'the glass of fashion and the mold of form.'"

Like everyone else who knew "that strange man," Boyers wondered why he suddenly resigned as governor, "leaving behind a bride of three months." Since he saw Houston as "powerfully built, wonderful in animal strength and vitality and of an ardent temperament," he believed he knew why the marriage failed.

Having experienced lovemaking among the Cherokees as an adolescent, Houston found his bride to be "cold." Neither she nor he could stomach this state of affairs; had she not suddenly departed, he almost certainly would have left her.

Leaving Nashville "with his rifle on his shoulder," Houston returned to the Cherokees who gave him a new name that meant "Big Drunk." Nevertheless, he succeeded in serving as mediator between his Cherokee family and their rivals, the Osages, Creeks, and Choctaws. He also married a Cherokee wife.

Perhaps because of Houston's unprecedented status among the Cherokee, Jackson approached him regarding Texas. At

*Houston during his
second period with
the Cherokees.*

least as early as 1822, Houston had invested in the Galveston
Bay and Texas Land Company. Jackson, firmly convinced that
Texas had been part of the Louisiana Purchase, was eager to
see the region become a part of the United States. He therefore
enlisted Houston's aid in opening communication with the
Comanches of Texas in December 1832.

Houston traveled part of the way with Georgia-born Jim
Bowie. By this time, Bowie owned land and a business near
San Antonio. Since he was an enthusiastic booster of Texas, he
may have persuaded Houston to take up residency. It seems to
have been the newcomer's own idea, however, to convert to
Roman Catholicism and consider Mexican citizenship.

To his cousin, he wrote, "Texas is the finest portion of the
Globe that has ever blessed my vision." Houston was granted a
headright on Karankawa Bay but chose to settle in Nacogdoches, living with another Tennessee acquaintance, Adolphus
Sterne. Both Sterne and Houston were delegates to the 1833 Convention, and Houston chaired the committee that drafted the

state constitution which Austin took to Mexico. In the meantime, Houston lost the Galveston Bay and Texas Land Company, filed for divorce from Eliza, and began to woo Anna Raguet.

The outbreak of the Texas revolution, however, saw him at the head of troops from Nacogdoches, marching west. The November Consultation of 1835 appointed Houston as commander in chief of the Texas army but failed to do anything substantive about raising an army. At the head of a volunteer army, he moved to Goliad and dispatched Bowie and a number of riders to San Antonio to inspect the garrison and possibly abandon it.

Houston, meanwhile, was drawn into the political processes of the independence movement and founding a government as well as organizing an army. The fall of the Alamo and the loss of Goliad, however, caused him to order his army to retreat in the face of the disasters. The army was undisciplined and untrained, incapable of engaging the Mexican army in the field. By withdrawing, Houston could enlist volunteers along the way and take advantage of some geographical barriers. Wherever he camped, he drilled his soldiers. By the end of March 1836 he had a force of fourteen hundred men.

At the same time Gen. Antonio López de Santa Anna had overseen the fall of the Alamo and the execution of the Texas garrison at Goliad. According to his best intelligence, this was the core of the Texas resistance. Sensing that there was no military threat from the Texans, Santa Anna divided his army into five columns and pursued the American colonists and destroyed their towns.

Houston continued to pull back, his progress impeded only by the flood of refugees eastward. He had no plan of attack other than knowing that the Mexican army was intent on destroying his army on the field. His only hope was if Santa Anna erred.

The Mexican president-general headed one of the five columns and pursued the seat of the Texas government relentlessly. Torching the town of Harrisburg and marching on New Washington, he turned his column to the northwest and suddenly trapped Houston's small army between the San Jacinto River and Buffalo Bayou. In so doing, he allowed a smaller force to advance in front of the Texans. At this moment, Houston had superior numbers, and both armies were hampered by marshland. Fortune smiled on Houston,

*President Samuel
Houston of the
Republic of Texas.*

though, when one of his scouts captured a Mexican courier
with dispatches containing Santa Anna's planned movements.

Houston's soldiers were frustrated by their constant retreat;
they were angry and murderous. The battle lasted only a few
minutes, but the bloodletting continued for the rest of the day.
Few cries for mercy were heeded.

At the end of the day, Houston sat propped against a tree,
nursing a wound to his right ankle and listening to the reports
of the dead and wounded. More than six hundred Mexican
corpses lay on the field and almost as many had surrendered.
Texan losses were two killed and twenty-four wounded, but
Houston added the eight hundred who died at the Alamo and
Goliad to the total cost of Texas independence.

The runaway bridegroom found a new home in the Lone
Star State and played a significant role in its independence and
later annexation by the United States. Houston became the first
president of the new republic. Later he was the first U.S. senator from the new state, and he was serving as governor at the
outbreak of the Civil War.

13
Joanna Troutman

The Betsy Ross of Texas

With a bag of flour slung across her shoulder instead of nestling between her hip and arm, Joanna Troutman stepped from the only general store in Knoxville, Georgia, and headed toward the big inn operated by her father.

As soon as she was judged to be out of earshot, a codger slouched on the whittling bench observed, "She sure ain't much to look at."

"No," responded a comrade as he shifted his quid of tobacco from his left to his right cheek. "A looker she ain't, but they say nobody in Crawford County can sew a straighter seam. Besides," he added, "her pa owns five thousand acres of the best land hereabouts."

Eighteen miles west of Macon, Knoxville had provided several of the volunteers making up Col. William Ward's company en route to Texas to fight the Mexicans. Inordinately proud of their emblem, these soldiers would fight anyone who questioned Joanna Troutman's skill as a seamstress.

Headed toward Montgomery, Alabama, the group known as the Macon Volunteers paused for a day or two in Columbus, Georgia. There a tall young lieutenant scribbled "Nov. 23rd, 1835" on a sheet of paper addressed to "Miss Joanna" and wrote:

> Colonel Ward brought your handsome and appropriate flag [featuring a single blue star] as a present to the Georgia Volunteers in the cause of "Texas and Liberty." I was fearful, from the shortness of the time, that you would not be able to finish it as

85

ARCHIVES & INFORMATION SERVICES DIVISION, TEXAS STATE LIBRARY

*Joanna Troutman
achieved fleeting fame
as maker of the Lone
Star flag.*

tastefully as you would wish, but I assure you, without an emotion of flattery, that it is *beautiful*, and with us its value is enhanced by the recollection of the *donor*.

I thank you for the honor of being made the medium of presentation to the company, and if they are what every true Georgian ought to be, your flag shall yet wave over fields of Victory in defiance of Despotism.

I hope the proud day may soon arrive, and while your star presides none can doubt of success.

Very respectfully, your friend,
Hugh McLeod

According to John C. Butler of Macon, "This patriotic banner was the first one ever made in Crawford County." He described the silk flag as being "in the history of the rising Republic of Texas, renowned as the first flag of the 'Lone Star' that was unfurled upon its soil."

Before the Georgia volunteers reached their destination, Sarah Dodson made a flag for another Georgia militia company, one in which her husband fought at San Antonio de

Bexar. Her long red-white-and-blue tricolor featured a white five-pointed star on a blue field. Hugh McLeod's letter offers some credibility to the contention that Joanna Troutman's flag was the earliest emblem to be produced, despite the fact that Sarah Dodson's was the first to be flown in Texas. Today some Texans might question the story from Crawford County because they would wonder why a Lone Star flag would have been made in Georgia.

Very early in the Texas struggle for independence from Mexico, intense interest was aroused in Georgia. Public meetings were held throughout the state, and several towns were selected as recruitment centers. Much of this flurry of excitement about Texas stemmed from the work of James W. Fannin.

A native of Columbus, Georgia, Fannin had attended the U.S. Military Academy at West Point before migrating to Texas in 1834. After clashing with the Mexican army at Gonzales in 1835, Fannin recruited and formed the Brazos Guards. Concurrently, he fired a series of letters to friends far to the east. His letters home led Ward and the others to raise companies of volunteers to aid Fannin and his comrades.

The Macon Volunteers proudly displayed their flag as they boarded the steamer *Benjamin Franklin* at Mobile, Alabama. At that time they were simply a body of enthusiasts who had selected their own officers in the tradition of local militias—they were not an authorized military unit. The law forbade a formal organization until they reached the Republic of Texas, which was outside the jurisdiction of the United States.

Aboard the steamer *Pennsylvania* for a second leg of their journey, Ward and his men did not reach Velasco at the mouth of the Brazos River until late in December. Back home, public interest in Texas and enthusiasm for its fight for independence remained high. On April 21, the day of the all-important battle of San Jacinto, the *Macon Telegraph* informed readers: "Captain Robert S. Patton, of this place, expects to leave for Texas in a few days, with all the men and means that he can carry to their assistance. Any individuals that are disposed to go with him can do so, free of expense, if they will report themselves without delay."

William A. O. Wadworth of Columbus is believed to have been the first to lead Georgia volunteers into Texas. His original company of thirty-five men grew in size as they passed

This Kentucky-made flag was the only emblem of Texans at San Jacinto.

through Alabama and Mississippi. At Milledgeville, J. C. Winn formed and led a third company of thirty-six Georgians.

Ward's company took a great deal of pride in having the distinction of Joanna Troutman's white silk flag with the single five-pointed blue star. Two mottoes were embroidered on the banner. One was the famous slogan of the American Revolution, "Liberty or Death." The other was devised by a Latinist and proclaimed *Ubi libertas habitat, ibi nostra patria est* (Where liberty dwells, there is my country).

Upon reaching Velasco, Ward and his men joined forces with the other two Georgia companies. On December 23, they organized as the Georgia Battalion, elected Ward as their major, and offered their services to Fannin. There they unfurled their flag on January 8, 1836, using the flagpole from which the Texas flag of independence already flew. Fannin had defeated a Mexican force at Concepcion and welcomed the newcomers into his command.

When news of the Texas Declaration of Independence reached Velasco, the banner of the Lone Star was fluttering in the wind. At sunset, when the flag was lowered, the fragile silk became entangled with the halyard and was ripped to shreds. The 150 men in Fannin's Georgia Battalion comprised one-third of his strength. Their enthusiasm was such that tradition says they insisted on preserving a portion of Joanna Troutman's flag. They took it with them to Goliad, where it is believed to have been flying when the Americans were forced to evacuate that post.

When Gen. Antonio López de Santa Anna was captured at San Jacinto in April 1836, the victorious Texans gleefully divided his property and goods among themselves. An elaborate silver service was part of that cache. Probably at the behest of Gen. Thomas Jefferson Rusk, the heavy Mexican-made spoons and forks were shipped to Joanna Troutman as a token of gratitude for the flag she had designed. Regardless of any competing claims, the first congress of the Republic of Texas made the Lone Star flag official and also imprinted the symbol on the republic's early currency.

In 1839 Joanna Troutman married an Alabama attorney and went to live at his Elmwood Plantation on the Flint River. She was locally renowned as the seventeen-year-old girl who had conceived and created the Lone Star flag that was carried to Texas by the Macon Volunteers.

Not until 1913 did Texas lawmakers turn their attention to the question of the creator of the Lone Star flag. After spirited debate, they enacted a measure naming Joanna Troutman as "the Betsy Ross of Texas" and erected a full-size statue of the Georgia seamstress on the capitol grounds. During the administration of Gov. Oscar B. Colquitt, a native of Georgia who had been reared in northeast Texas, Joanna's remains were removed from her family's burial ground and reinterred in the Texas State Cemetery in Austin.

14

James W. Fannin

Sudden Death at Goliad

The Mexican settlers at the village of Gonzales welcomed the first Americans who came to them. Not far from the Gulf of Mexico, almost due east of San Antonio, the village was so isolated that their spokesmen requested a cannon for their protection. In 1831 a little swivel gun was sent from San Antonio de Bexar.

Four years later, with numerous Americans now living in the area, Gen. Domingo de Ugartechea demanded that the village relinquish the gun. Instead of obeying the order, the Texans-by-choice loaded their weapon and on October 2, 1835, fired it in the general direction of Ugartechea's troops. The skirmish that followed launched the Texas revolution against Mexico.

Sam Houston, who was at Gonzales, realized that retaliation was likely to be swift. Hence the following winter he ordered his followers to evacuate all the nearby communities around Goliad, south of the site at which the revolution had begun. Its location on the south bank of the San Antonio River gave it a strong defensive position.

Georgia-born James W. Fannin, who had spent two years at the U.S. Military Academy, was in command of fewer than three hundred men at Goliad. He had moved his wife and two daughters to Texas in 1834, and because of his military training was soon made an officer.

Directed to evacuate his outpost, Fannin decided to destroy the little fortress at Goliad and cut his way through the enemy forces separating him from Houston's army near the Colorado River. He started on March 18, but the men from Goliad had

James W. Fannin headed a force at Goliad that was almost twice the size of the Alamo garrison. He surrendered in the face of superior numbers, but his men were massacred nonetheless.

ARCHIVES & INFORMATION SERVICES DIVISION, TEXAS STATE LIBRARY

proceeded only a few miles before they were confronted by a vastly superior Mexican force.

The Americans formed a hollow square to defend themselves on all sides and fought valiantly until nightfall. During this fierce engagement, Fannin's force suffered sixty-seven casualties, but he calculated that the enemy had lost at least six hundred men.

The arrival of fresh troops and artillery led Fannin to negotiate terms for surrender with Gen. José Urrea. Fannin was given a fourfold set of promises: all prisoners of war would be marched back to Goliad, the American volunteers would be transported to New Orleans at the expense of the Mexican government, officers could keep their sidearms, and the fighting men who resided in and around Goliad would have their property restored to them.

Upon surrendering, according to a contemporary account, "the Texan army was deprived of every article of defense, even to their pocket-knives." Soon they found themselves imprisoned in the Mission la Bahia, close to Goliad, where

In the battle of Goliad, the Texas settlers didn't have a chance against an overwhelming Mexican force.

they were given "an allowance of food hardly sufficient to support life."

Several days earlier, Fannin had sent Capt. Amon B. King and a company of men to Refugio, nearly thirty miles away. When they arrived there on March 11, 1836, they expected to defend the outpost, only fifteen miles from the coast. Soon, however, they received orders to evacuate civilians and guard them as they traveled toward Goliad. King found the order impossible to obey, so he took refuge in a mission and dispatched a courier with a plea for help.

Long before his message reached Goliad, King was forced to surrender to General Urrea. Six hours later, all of the Americans and their Mexican allies were shot.

Unaware of this, Fannin responded to King's request for reinforcements by dispatching Col. William Ward and his Georgia Battalion to Refugio. Samuel G. Hardaway, a sixteen-year-old member of the battalion, later wrote an account of their mission. Having been ordered back to Goliad, they fought two bloody battles against an estimated fourteen hundred Mexicans. With their ammunition exhausted, they surrendered on the third day of fighting and became prisoners of war who were also herded into La Bahia Mission.

Maj. William P. Miller of Tennessee headed nearly seventy volunteers rushing to the aid of the Texans and landed at Copano about the middle of March. He and his men became prisoners almost as soon as they set foot on land and were herded to Goliad and the prison improvised from the mission buildings.

Later in the month, Urrea is believed to have received orders from Gen. Antonio López de Santa Anna, who headed both the Mexican army and the government. It is possible but highly unlikely that Urrea acted on his own. Whatever the case, a detachment of guards roused the prisoners early on the morning of Palm Sunday, March 27, 1836. Four surgeons and four assistants were brusquely moved aside; they assumed that their services would be needed in an improvised hospital. A few other prisoners were ordered to step aside also; they would be useful as laborers.

Dividing all the rest, except the Tennesseans, into four companies, Urrea's guards directed them to march out of the mission. "They proceeded in file," says an early account of the day, "and as they came within range of men stationed on each side of the road, a fire of musketry was opened upon them."

S. T. Brown managed to escape the volley of rifle fire. He said later that he almost regretted having saved his life when he "heard the cries of dying men and saw the sickening flow of their blood." Soon recaptured and returned to Goliad, Brown was astonished to find that "all eighty-two men from Tennessee were alive, not having been included in the mass execution."

According to Brown, Urrea's firing squads carefully avoided hitting high-ranking officers among their foes until all common soldiers were on the ground. If Brown's account is accurate, Ward was ordered to kneel before his captors after his men had been shot and was told that his life would be spared if he obeyed. He refused, saying that he had no desire to live after watching the execution of his comrades.

Once Ward was dead, Fannin is believed to have been the only man still on his feet. Tradition contends that "the fearless Goliad commandant bared his breast to the Mexicans and told them to shoot him through the heart, not in the head."

"Remember Goliad!" by Artist Norman Price.

A few of the wounded survived and managed to escape, hence the exact number who perished in what became known as the Goliad Massacre is not known. Most accounts suggest that at least 340 unarmed men were killed. Muster rolls of Ward's battalion indicate that 80 of the dead were natives of a single eastern state—Georgia.

When news of the atrocity crossed the Mississippi River, the initial public reaction was disbelief. As the truth became known, unmitigated horror gave way to rage. Because of the horrors that occurred at Goliad, it was natural that Sam Houston's little army charged the Mexican army at San Jacinto shouting "Remember Goliad!" along with "Remember the Alamo!"

Part 4
Raw Courage

In Texas lore there is no better example of courage than the men who fought and died in the Alamo.

15
Theodore H. Barrett
The Last Hurrah

Within six months of Abraham Lincoln's ordering a blockade of all ports in the recently seceded states, Federal warships were implementing it. As flag officer of the West Gulf Blockading Squadron, David G. Farragut turned his attention to the Texas coast. He took note of a potentially vulnerable spot just north of the border with Mexico.

On February 24, 1862, Farragut issued special orders to Comdr. Samuel Swartout of the USS *Hartford*: "On the first fine day for the purpose you will land a party in your boats with the howitzers and take possession of the point of land which best commands the entrance to Brazos Santiago. Once [the place is] taken, you will run down and communicate with Mr. Chase, our consul at Tampico, or send the vessel sent to assist you and learn the best mode of intercepting the trade of the Confederates going on between that place and Texas."

Farragut's plan to close the inlet to the Confederacy's important cotton port of Brownsville was unfulfilled until November 1863, when Federal troops seized Brazos Santiago Island—now known as Brazos. Under the protection of Yankee naval guns, workmen quickly built a semipermanent base on the island. Eventually the barracks erected here housed about 950 men, and at least one warship was usually anchored nearby.

More than a year before Brazos Santiago was occupied by Union troops, Maj. Gen. John B. Magruder was given command of the Confederate Military District of Texas. One of his subordinates, Brig. Gen. James E. Slaughter, was charged with the special responsibility for the coast, yet no Rebel force within 150 miles of Brownsville was considered strong enough to wrest the island from the North once a Union force was garrisoned there.

In 1864, Confederate Col. John S. Ford, admiringly known to his men as "Rip," led a secret expedition to the Rio Grande and established a camp about 165 miles from Brownsville. With money being scarce in the South, when Ford requested funds, he received two hundred bales of cotton to finance his enterprise.

By the time Ford had bargained away the last of his cotton, it was clear that U. S. Grant's Union army in the East was squeezing the vitality out of Robert E. Lee's Army of Northern Virginia. In Texas, Union Maj. Gen. Lew Wallace began negotiating terms for an honorable surrender with Slaughter and Ford. After news of Lee's surrender reached Texas in late April 1865, the negotiated terms were submitted to Union Maj. Gen. John Walker. Surprisingly, the terms were rejected.

Perhaps as early as April 20, Ford knew that Lee had surrendered. He and his aides recognized that the war was over and began making plans to return to their homes. Col. Theodore H. Barrett, commander of the Union post at Brazos Santiago, received telegraphic word about Appomattox a bit earlier, possibly on Good Friday, April 15, about the same time he learned that John Wilkes Booth had assassinated President Lincoln.

Barrett was an insecure officer. Described by his subordinates as "puffed up by ambition," he had spent the war years in obscure places. One of his officers later wrote the *New York Times* that the colonel's eagerness "to establish for himself some notoriety" led him to issue orders that his soldiers considered strange.

On the evening of May 11, 250 men of the Sixty-second U.S. Colored Infantry and 50 unmounted men of the Second Texas Cavalry were directed from Brazos Santiago to the mainland. Ostensibly, their primary objective was horse hunting, but the soldiers knew they were expected to meet and vanquish the only Rebel force within striking distance. Colonel Ford's ragged and hungry men were believed to be near Palmito Ranch—whose name was frequently incorrectly listed as Palmetto—about fifteen miles from the Federal-held island.

It was easy for Barrett to issue such orders, but it was hard for his men to follow them. A severe storm slowed their crossing of the Boca Chica inlet, so the Union soldiers had to march

Condederate Gen. James E. Slaughter, here shown in a postwar photo, commanded Southern troops at Palmito Ranch. After the engagement, he led a few diehards to Mexico, but he eventually returned to Mobile, Alabama, and for a time served as postmaster.

nearly all night to reach their objective before dawn. According to Barrett's report to Maj. Gen. Lorenzo Thomas, early on the morning of May 12 his troops, under Lt. Col. David Branson, "attacked a strong outpost of the rebels at Palmetto Ranch, Tex., on the banks of the Rio Grande."

Confederate accounts give the same information about the timing of this first encounter between the opposing forces, but subsequent events were treated quite differently. Eyewitness reports of actions during the following thirty-six hours vary wildly, with both the Federals and the Rebels claiming victory.

According to Barrett, Ford and his men "were driven in confusion from their position," with the result that their "camp, camp equipage, and stores" were captured. Without explaining why, the Federal troops retired to a nearby ranch to camp for the night. Sometime after midnight this force was augmented by the Thirty-fourth Indiana Infantry. If the count was accurate, a force of more than five hundred Union soldiers prepared to meet the enemy.

Barrett assumed command from Branson and turned back toward Palmito Ranch, which had been "reoccupied by the rebels" while the Federal troops had established their camp. He claimed to have driven the Confederate cavalry from the field at about 8:00 A.M. With Palmito Ranch in his possession, he ordered the buildings and supplies destroyed. His report then stated: "A detachment was here sent back to Brazos Santiago with our wounded and the prisoners and captures of the day previous. The remainder of the force was ordered to advance. Nearly the entire forenoon was spent in skirmishing. The enemy, though taking advantage of every favorable position, was everywhere easily driven back. Early in the afternoon a sharp engagement took place, which, being in the chaparral, was attended with comparatively little loss to us." Having driven the enemy several miles, Barrett reported, he decided to permit his weary men to rest before returning to "a hill about a mile from Palmetto Ranch."

There, about 4:00 P.M., Barrett reported that Ford and his men "now largely re-enforced, again reappeared in our front." The Confederate cavalry had bolstered its force with six 12-pounder fieldpieces. Lacking artillery of their own, the Union force retreated toward its fortified base behind a skirmish line "nearly three-quarters of a mile in length, and reaching to the river bank."

This line, manned by members of the Sixty-second U.S. Colored Infantry, held for three hours. Gradually falling back "with precision and in perfect order," Barrett reported that when his force returned to its base "our entire loss in killed, wounded, and captured was 4 officers and 111 men."

The adjutant-general's attention was called to the fact that Barrett's report constituted a description "of the last actual conflict between hostile forces in the great rebellion." In a separate report, Lieutenant Colonel Branson sounded a different note of triumph: "The entire operation demonstrated the fact that the negro soldiers can march; also that this regiment can keep order in the ranks and be depended upon under trying circumstances."

Many details of the Barrett report, however, were challenged by the Confederates. Colonel Ford had arrived on the scene around 3:00 P.M. His summary of the action, here greatly abbreviated, differs significantly from that of Barrett:

> I found myself in the presence of 800 infantry. I had 300 cavalry and a light battery. Having made a reconnaissance and

determined to attack, skirmishers were advanced. The artillery opened fire before the enemy were aware we had guns in the field.

Very soon Captain [W. N.] Robinson charged with impetuosity. As was expected, the Yankee skirmishers were captured, and the enemy were retreating at a run. The guns pursued at a gallop; the shouting men pressed to the front, occupying the hill adjacent to the road, and fired in security from behind the crest. The enemy endeavored to hold various points, but were driven from them. The pursuit lasted for nearly 7 miles, when the artillery horses were greatly fatigued; some of them had given out, and the cavalry horses were jaded.

After having withdrawn a short distance, Brigadier-General Slaughter arrived and assumed command. The enemy were followed within a mile of Brazos island. In this affair the enemy lost 25 or 30 killed and wounded and 113 prisoners.

Except for Barrett's and Branson's reports, all eyewitness accounts agree that Palmito Ranch was a resounding Confederate victory in which the Federals suffered numerous casualties. Pvt. John J. Williams of the Thirty-fourth Indiana is the only Union soldier known to have been killed while the running battle was in progress. More than a year later, the adjutant general of Indiana calculated the losses of the Thirty-fourth as "eighty-two in killed, wounded and prisoners." For the Southerners, Slaughter reported his losses at "four or five who were severely wounded."

Confederate Col. O. M. Roberts of the Eleventh Texas was not present during the struggle, but discussed it during May 1865 with Ford and two other eyewitnesses, W. G. Miller and J. H. Moore. The future governor of Texas concluded, "It is not known why this battle was fought."

Although the motives behind the fight at Palmito Ranch are not known, its significant result may be summarized in Barrett's concluding remarks: "The last volley of the war [was fired by the] Sixty-second U.S. Colored Infantry about sunset on the 13th of May, 1865."

Of course, others claimed to have fired the last shots of the war at Palmito Ranch. Slaughter declared that he rode into the muddy water behind the retreating Federals and emptied his pistol at their backs. According to one of the Confederate officers, however, a Union warship fired on the Southerners as

*Pvt. John J. Williams of the
Thirty-fourth Indiana is
reputed to be the last man
killed during the Civil War.
He was the only casualty
during the running battle
at Palmito Ranch.*

they approached Brazos Island. In response, the officer noted, "A seventeen-year-old trooper blazed away in the direction of the exploded shell with his Enfield rifle. The firing ceased. The last gun had been fired."

Just as there is conflicting evidence as to who fired the first shot of the war at Charleston Harbor, there is no way to determine who fired the last shot of the war. What is certain is that an obscure Union officer, whether out of zeal or unholy ambition, memorialized an otherwise easily forgotten site. In addition to that, the Confederate victory at Palmito Ranch gives lasting support to the frequently voiced claim that Texans never lost a Civil War battle on Texas soil.

16
Travis, Bowie, and Crockett

The Alamo

Few American pioneers in Texans had a major quarrel with Mexican rule when they first arrived. By 1833, however, most of them wanted the same kind of freedom they had enjoyed in the United States. Their armed revolt was initially designed to put an end to military dictatorship, and among many of them independence did not have a high priority.

Things changed rapidly when Gen. Antonio López de Santa Anna gained dictatorial power in Mexico and made plans to send an army of occupation into the state of Coahuila, which included the Texas province. Meeting at San Felipe de Austin late in 1835, leaders of the colonists passed a resolution saying that they would fight "in defense of Mexico's federal constitution of 1824." Soon they established a provisional government, complete with a council and a governor.

Six months before these events unfolded, the American settlers had defeated a small force of Mexicans who hoped to capture a rusty cannon mounted at Gonzales. This victory set many of Stephen Austin's followers on fire, and they persuaded him to lead them to San Antonio to take over the town. The city's population was then close to two thousand, with a large majority of residents being Mexicans.

Late in October 1833, the colonists had won another small victory at Concepción Mission when they drove a body of Mexican troops into San Antonio. After a siege that was followed by hand-to-hand fighting, the Mexican garrison surrendered and withdrew across the Rio Grande.

With San Antonio considered to be firmly in their hands, some colonists went home. Numerous others joined an expedition to seize the faraway port of Matamoros and to capture a herd of horses known to be near it.

On orders from Provisional Gov. Henry Smith in January 1836, William Barrett Travis was ordered to occupy San Antonio, and he led about thirty military veterans to the town. Only days after his arrival, Col. James C. Neill relinquished command to the newcomer so he could care for his family.

Soon after taking over, Travis sent an urgent dispatch to Governor Smith, describing his position briefly and saying: "We are determined to sustain this post as long as there is a man left, because we consider death preferable to disgrace. Should we receive no reinforcements, I am determined to defend it to the last."

Travis knew that his small force of 125 to 150 men was outnumbered nearly thirty to one by the approaching Mexican army. He had no illusions about the outcome of a battle.

Across the San Antonio River from the main section of the town, a three-acre compound was popularly known as the Alamo. No one remembered when the first barracks for Mexican cavalry had been erected there, but by 1835 it had been converted into a fort of sorts. Once the conversion was completed, its outer walls of stone and a series of ditches made it seem easy to defend.

Abandoned when Mexican troops were forced from the town, the Alamo was occupied by Travis and his men. They had about a score of cannon, ranging in size from several 6-pounders to a single 18-pounder. When the expected attack by the Mexicans came, the Alamo defenders would rely on their artillery to drive the attackers away.

Receiving word that the Mexican army was approaching San Antonio, Travis and his men dug in during the month of February 1836. Most of these men were new arrivals to this land of opportunity, having been there only a few months. A surprising number—probably as many as forty—had come from Great Britain and Europe; nearly all of the rest had been born and reared in the eastern United States. A handful of Travis's followers pulled out of the Alamo, but his force was strengthened by three or four Mexican civilians.

Jim Bowie, believed to have been born in Kentucky during the last decade of the previous century, had acquired a reputation for fierce hand-to-hand fighting and the honorary title of

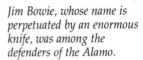

Jim Bowie, whose name is perpetuated by an enormous knife, was among the defenders of the Alamo.

colonel. His arrival at the improvised fort in January was greeted by a spontaneous cheer from the Texas garrison. Bowie's presence was buttressed by his infamous knife whose blade was eight or nine inches long and about two inches wide. Travis (for the regular army) and Bowie (for the volunteers) formed a joint command for the garrison.

Davy Crockett reached San Antonio during the second week of February at the head of a dozen men from Tennessee. He was probably the best-known man among the defenders. It was alleged that his strength was waning fast since he was in the last stage of tuberculosis.

Like all who agreed to stay with Travis, Bowie and Crockett knew that if a siege should come they would be forced to survive on corn and fresh beef from a few cattle they had seized. Supplies of both foodstuffs were limited, and the Texans had no salt. Neither did they have coffee with which to wash down their tasteless meals.

A Texan scout is believed to have seen the sun glistening upon Mexican armor near the Medina River on February 21.

Effectively isolated from other English-speaking settlers, the self-appointed garrison of the Alamo was only twenty miles away from the long columns of Santa Anna's soldiers.

It took the slow-moving Mexican force two days to reach San Antonio and to invest the town. A handful of Mexican women and children hurried to the Alamo to take refuge. There they found that the wife and small daughter of Almeron Dickinson had preceded them to the place of sanctuary.

During the middle of the afternoon, one of Santa Anna's aides supervised the raising of a flag at perhaps the highest point in the town—the tower of the parish church. Devoid of symbols, the flag needed none; its blood-red color was known to be a signal that if the Mexicans should meet resistance, they would give no quarter.

As soon as the flag was pointed out to Travis, he fired a symbolic shot. Then he sat down and drafted an address to "the People of Texas and all the Americans in the World." Taken from the Alamo by a volunteer courier on February 24 and destined for the eyes of Governor Smith, General Houston, and the provisional council, the dispatch combined defiance of the enemy with a plea for speedy aid:

> Fellow Citizens & Compatriots
> I am besieged by a thousand or more of the Mexicans under Santa Anna. I have sustained a continual bombardment & cannonade for 24 hours & have not lost a man. The enemy has demanded a surrender at discretion, otherwise the garrison are to be put to the sword if the fort is taken. I have answered the demand with a cannon shot, and our flag still waves proudly from the walls. I shall never surrender nor retreat. Then, I call on you in the name of Liberty, of patriotism, & of everything dear to the American character, to come to our aid with all dispatch. The enemy is receiving reinforcements daily & will no doubt increase to three or four thousand in four or five days. If this call is neglected, I am determined to sustain myself as long as possible & die like a soldier who never forgets what is due to his own honor & that of his country.

A few reinforcements answered Travis's appeal and managed to penetrate enemy lines and enter the Alamo grounds, bringing the total strength of the defenders to about 189 men.

The Alamo was only a small part of the area defended by Travis's regulars and Bowie's and Crockett's volunteers.

Travis probably knew that his plea was largely useless; the nearest Texas settlement was a three-day ride away, at Gonzales. Even if some Texans there should mount up as soon as they heard the news, they could not reach San Antonio in time to affect the coming struggle to the death.

Surrounded and besieged, the Alamo defenders remained cheerful and hopeful for the first few days. Things took a turn for the worse when Santa Anna's artillery arrived and began a sporadic firing from dawn until dark. After midnight on Sunday, March 5, a thunderous cannonade sounded as though the Mexicans had enough big guns to demolish the thick stone walls at will.

Well before daylight on Monday, the Mexicans launched a massive charge that wilted when the Alamo's cannon began to fire. The attackers fell back but soon returned, only to be stopped by the defenders' heavy fire. At the third assault, the

The third and final assault upon the Alamo breached the walls and overwhelmed the fort's defenders.

walls were breached and the Texas artillery became useless. Those defenders who still survived were scattered about the bare plaza of the Alamo, approximately as big as a city block.

As long as they could draw their breath, pull a trigger, or use their weapons as clubs, the Texans continued to offer a fierce resistance. Nevertheless, all of the defenders were killed. Legend has it that Bowie, too ill to stand, fired sporadically from a cot that sat inside the little church.

Several noncombatants were spared, including Susanna Dickenson, the wife of one of the defenders, Susanna's baby, and a servant of Travis. Partly to reinforce his goal of terrorizing colonists in Texas, Santa Anna released this small party to inform the rebellious Texans of the fate of the defenders.

The only accounts of the battle of the Alamo came from those who were spared and, aside from the reports submitted to Mexico City, second- or third-hand accounts describe the action within the besieged mission. A Mexican officer's diary was discovered in 1978 which alleges that Crockett and possibly as many as five other Texans surrendered to end the fighting in the mission. The diary notes that these prisoners were summarily executed on Santa Anna's orders. It is known, however, that once his victory was won, Santa Anna ordered that the bodies of the Texans be burned.

According to a very early Mexican account, 182 bodies were placed on a huge pile that was ignited in the late afternoon of March 5. Contemporary historians are of the opinion that the number of men who died in defense of the Alamo was somewhere between 150 and 200. If the higher estimate is correct, it means that the price exacted by the Texans was approximately eight to one, since about 1,600 Mexican soldiers died.

The small Alamo garrison had held off the Mexican army for almost two weeks, delaying Santa Anna's eastward march and giving the Texans more time to organize politically and militarily. In the history of the United States, the Alamo defenders have come to be revered as a supreme example of the virtues of unyielding courage and heroic self-sacrifice.

17
Barbara Jordan

Captive Listener

On the evening of July 25, 1974, chairman Peter Rodino of the Judiciary Committee of the U.S. House of Representatives said, "I recognize the gentlelady from Texas, Ms. Jordan, for the purpose of general debate, not to exceed a period of fifteen minutes."

After a customary statement of thanks, attorney Barbara Charline Jordan of Houston began speaking in a resonant voice that many who were watching their television sets agreed was "hypnotic" in its power.

Jordan was the only African-American woman on the committee charged with deciding whether or not to draw up articles of impeachment against President Richard M. Nixon. In this unique situation, she began by saying, "Earlier today, we heard the beginning of the Preamble to the Constitution of the United States, 'We, the people . . .' It is a very eloquent beginning. But when that document was completed on the seventeenth of September 1787, I was not included in that 'We, the people.' I felt somehow for many years that George Washington and Alexander Hamilton just left me out by mistake."

Jordan's powerful and melodic voice would have captivated listeners regardless of what she said. After her brief reference to racial inequality in the nation's Constitution, she continued, "Today, I am an inquisitor. My faith in the Constitution is whole, it is complete, it is total. I am not going to sit here and be an idle spectator to the diminution, the subversion, the destruction of the Constitution."

After a brief analysis of the legal basis for the impeachment process, she cited President Woodrow Wilson, once a teacher of public law, who said, "Indignation so great as to overthrow party interest may secure a conviction; nothing else can." Then the representative from Texas turned to James Madison, who wrote, "If the President be connected in any suspicious manner with any person . . . he may be impeached." Having demonstrated that she had done her homework with care, Jordan ended her speech with a challenge: "If the impeachment provision in the Constitution of the United States will not reach the offenses charged here, perhaps the eighteenth-century Constitution should be abandoned to a twentieth-century paper shredder. Has the president committed offenses and planned and directed and acquiesced in a course of conduct which the Constitution will not tolerate? That is the question. We should now forthwith proceed to answer the question. It is reason, and not passion, which must guide our deliberations, guide our debate, and guide our decision."

Jordan's challenge electrified the nation. The *Washington Post* published the complete text of her opening statement, here greatly abbreviated. Both *Time* and *Newsweek* featured her message and her face; as the hearing progressed, the Texan's voice became instantly recognizable to millions.

Three articles of impeachment having been adopted, Nixon resigned on August 9, 1974, the only chief executive to take such a course of action. By the time the vice president, Gerald Ford, succeeded him, Barbara Jordan was being talked about for the nation's highest office.

She ignored letters of praise for her work on the Judiciary Committee and refused requests for interviews. "I am here to represent some of the people of Texas," she said repeatedly. "That is my sole purpose and goal." When colleagues urged her to seek the vice presidential nomination at the upcoming Democratic National Convention, she issued a statement saying, "I will not allow, sanction, or approve in any manner whatsoever my name being placed in nomination; that is final."

Nonetheless, she accepted an invitation to share the platform at the 1976 convention with Sen. John Glenn. After her speech there, television commentators and print reporters reminded the public that Jordan was the first woman to go to Congress from the Deep South since the Reconstruction era. Many quoted her concluding words: "I am going to close by quoting

Barbara Jordan functioned as "governor for a day" on June 10, 1972.

a Republican president, and I ask that as you listen to these words of Abraham Lincoln to relate them to the concept of a national community in which every last one of us participates: 'As I would not be a slave, so I would not be a master.' This expresses my idea of democracy."

At this point in her career, the lawmaker could have had any political plum she wanted. Instead of seeking and accepting one, she left Congress to teach at the University of Texas. It is uncertain if she then knew she had multiple sclerosis.

Barbara Jordan was born in 1936, just four years after African Americans in Texas were first permitted to vote in democratic primaries. She was deeply influenced by Houston's Good Hope Baptist Church, in which she remained active all her life.

At Texas Southern University, she was a member of the debating team for four years before her 1956 graduation, magna cum laude. By then she had applied for admission to

Boston University to study law to the surprise and consternation of her father, who warned her that "lawyering is no
profession for a girl to be in."

After receiving her doctor of laws degree in 1959, Jordan
passed the bar examination in Massachusetts because she was
not sure she wanted to return to segregated Texas. Soon, however, she concluded that, regardless of the consequences, she
must spend her future where she had grown up. She initially
practiced law from the dining room table of the family home.

Knowing herself to be qualified for public office, she waged
unsuccessful campaigns for a seat in the Texas legislature in
1962 and 1964. Finally, she won in 1966 and became the first
black woman to go to the state senate.

Six years later she decided to enter the campaign for the
Eighteenth Congressional District of Texas. Situated in
downtown Houston, it comprised an electorate that was
approximately 70 percent black and 30 percent white.

Defeating three male opponents, Jordan won the Democratic nomination, which was tantamount to election. Had she
gone to Congress at any other time and had she not been
placed on the Judiciary Committee because of her legal background, the Houston woman might have had a mediocre
career in Washington.

When some quizzed her about her decision to become a
lawyer, she recounted the career of Phyllis Wheatley. "She was
the slave of a successful Boston tailor," Jordan said. "Some
time in the 1760s her owner discovered lines of poetry she had
written. At age fourteen, she won acclaim for her verse, and in
1773 became the first black American to write a book."

In Houston Jordan's school was named for the Massachusetts poet. "But that's not the heart of the story," she continued. "One day we were filed into chapel to hear a talk. I was
fourteen years old and had just read about the slave girl of
colonial days and what she accomplished. I wasn't eager to
listen to a female lawyer from Chicago, but had no choice in
the matter."

Soon, said Jordan, she found herself entranced by the
speaker who showed herself to be a master of both language
and law. Before the visitor ended her talk, Barbara had made
up her mind to become an attorney who might someday be in

114 A Treasury of Texas Tales

a position to exert an influence on behalf of the oppressed and the unfortunate.

That's how a captive listener made up her mind to become a lawyer—not dreaming that she would one day have her name bandied about as a presidential aspirant.

18
John Magruder
Hot Spot

In many respects, the action at Galveston reflects the whole of the Civil War in microcosm. Some of the major issues there concerned ship-to-shore engagements, acceptable use of flags of truce, and destruction of property to prevent capture.

The port of Galveston was important in establishing control of the western Gulf of Mexico. A long-running contest between the two sides began on July 3, 1861, when Union warships tried to establish a blockade. Before the end of the month, the Federal naval commander threatened to use his firepower on the town unless his demands were met.

Not until October 1862 was the island firmly controlled by Union naval forces. Capt. William B. Renshaw headed a squadron of four warships and a mortar boat when he informed the townspeople that he "would hoist the United States flag over the city of Galveston or over its ashes."

Just prior to Renshaw's ultimatum, Confederate Col. X. B. Debray warned, "Galveston cannot be defended, and a fight in the city would be a useless braggadocio against forty guns." Under these circumstances, said Debray, there was nothing to do but withdraw his small force from the city.

The two sides agreed on a four-day truce, which also allowed the citizens to decide to remain in Galveston or flee to the interior. Debray later reported: "I notified those disposed to remain that should the United States flag be hoisted over Galveston they would no longer be allowed to communicate with the continent and shall receive no supplies." He also warned the people that they would have to decide between

The blockade-runner Old Dominion *was a typical example of those that frequented Galveston.*

"abject submission and persecution plus insult." Some lacked the funds to pay for their relocation. Such persons, Debray said, would be taken to Houston at the expense of "the Government of the Confederate States."

Nearly all the civilians chose to leave. While their exodus was under way, a detachment of Union troops arrived from New Orleans, dispatched by Maj. Gen. Benjamin Butler. These men were to augment the grip of the naval forces on the city and, Butler hoped, "assist in recruiting Texas refugees [willing to fight in blue uniforms]."

On November 29, Brig. Gen. John Bankhead Magruder was assigned to command the Confederate military District of Texas, New Mexico, and Arizona. Immediately, he began making plans to drive the enemy from Galveston. This would be a formidable task as the Union vessels were known to be "armed with the latest improvements in long range guns."

Gen. John B. "Prince John" Magruder developed what seemed to be a foolhardy plan, but then carried it out successfully.

CENTURY WAR BOOK

Magruder's own forces on the mainland had only one small gun, a 10-pounder.

Rated at 822 tons, the USS *Westfield* had a 100-pounder Parrott rifle. The flagship of the Federal squadron, this warship also carried a 9-inch Dahlgren gun and four 8-inch guns that weighed 5,500 pounds each.

Less formidable but far more famous, the *Harriet Lane* was a one-time revenue cutter that had been transferred to the U.S. Navy in 1861. She carried three 9-inch guns, one 30-pounder rifle, and a bronze 12-pounder rifle.

The 507-ton USS *Owasco* was armed with a 20-pounder Parrott rifle, an 11-inch Dahlgren, and two 24-pounder howitzers. The battery of the USS *Clifton*, nearly twice as large as the *Owasco*, consisted of two 9-inch Dahlgrens, four 5,700-pound guns that fired 32-pound balls and shells, and one 30-pounder Parrott rifle. Rated at only 197 tons, Comdr. William B. Renshaw's fifth warship was the USS *Sachem*. Her armament consisted of a 20-pounder Parrott rifle and four 32-pounders. Two unarmed barks and a schooner completed the squadron facing Galveston.

The USS Westfield *boasted a formidable six-gun battery, but the vessel grounded and had to be blown up to prevent her falling into Rebel hands.*

Magruder personally led a midnight scouting expedition to inspect the forts that had been abandoned when Galveston was surrendered. He found all of these installations useless, but a railroad track leading to the city from Virginia Point seemed to be undamaged. In his account of his preparations, he wrote of this section of track: "By means of it I purposed to transport to a position near the enemy's fleet [the heaviest available guns]. By assembling all the movable artillery that could be collected together in the neighborhood, I hoped to acquire sufficient force to be able to expel the enemy's vessels from the harbor."

Twenty miles upriver from Galveston, two wood-burning steamers, the *Bayou City* and *Neptune*, were converted into gunboats by packing their decks with bales of cotton. The crews were armed with Enfield rifles, brought from Richmond by Magruder, and shotguns.

Confederate Capt. James Martin learned of the proposed expedition and eagerly joined it. A body of troops headed for Monroe, Louisiana, was expecting to wait ten days or more for transportation. Under the leadership of Col. James Reily, three hundred of them volunteered to take part in an assault that most military leaders would have considered hopeless.

Having decided to strike at midnight on December 31, Magruder deployed his forces skillfully. Personally leading the assault upon the center of the position held by Federal soldiers, he fired a gun signaling the attack. Although the moon had set, Federal ships just three hundred yards offshore could be seen by starlight. Soon, Magruder wrote, they "opened on us with a tremendous discharge of shell, which was followed with grape and canister."

The improvised Southern gunboats "came dashing down the harbor" and took the *Harriet Lane* as their first target. While rifle and shotgun fire was still pouring into the Union vessel, the cotton-clad *Neptune* was rammed and disabled. Aboard the *Bayou City*, her pilot made quick maneuvers that enabled her to escape serious damage. Almost simultaneously, the Federal flagship ran aground and the *Harriet Lane* was boarded. Confederate Maj. A. M. Lea was astonished to find that her badly wounded second in command was his son.

The Confederates offered Renshaw a truce during which, if he surrendered, he could depart with his men on one of his ships. Renshaw, however, did not want his flagship captured. When the crew had abandoned her, he ordered Lt. Comdr. Richard L. Law, commanding the *Clifton*, to withdraw all remaining vessels from the harbor, and he set his ship on fire. Renshaw "was himself accidentally blown up with it." The remaining Union vessels "gradually crept off with white flags still flying at their mastheads."

On land, all 260 men of the Sixty-second Massachusetts surrendered, raising the total of Federals killed or captured to 414. Magruder reported 26 killed and 117 wounded. On the afternoon of January 1, 1863, Lt. Albert M. Lea and another sailor were buried in a single grave "with Masonic and military honors."

The reaction of Union leaders constituted a mixture of consternation and rage. Rear Adm. David G. Farragut, head of the sixty-four vessels that made up the West Gulf Blockading Squadron, ordered Commo. H. H. Bell aboard the USS *Brooklyn*, along with three gunboats, to retake Galveston "or at any rate retake the *Harriet Lane*, if possible, and shell the troops out, if any appear."

Rear Adm. David D. Porter, commander of the Mississippi Squadron, wrote: "The disgraceful affair at Galveston has shaken the public confidence in our prestige. Five gunboats were sunk and dispersed by two river steamboats armed with one gun (which burst at the third fire) and filled only

The guns of the Harriet Lane *were much bigger than most field artillery used on land.*

with soldiers, the attack of the enemy being known the day before. It is too cowardly to place on paper."

In Virginia and in Texas, reactions to word of Magruder's victory were joyful. It took less than two months for the normally slow-moving Confederate Congress to pass a resolution of Thanks of Congress to Magruder, his chief officers, and "the Texan Rangers and soldiers engaged in the attack on and victory achieved at Galveston." A few weeks later, the legislature of Texas issued a joint resolution to thank the victors. Jefferson Davis conveyed his warm personal gratitude to the outgunned band of reckless men who succeeded in driving a Federal force from the most important port of the Lone Star State.

At war's end Galveston was the only major Southern port still in Confederate hands. Blockade-runners had managed to escape from the port as late as April 1864. Immense quantities of munitions, food, and other supplies flowed into the Confederacy as a result of Magruder's midnight attack upon a force vastly stronger than his own. Important as this factor was, the boost given to their morale by the recapture of Galveston was a key element in the decision of the Confederates to keep on fighting against apparently insuperable odds.

19
Dan Rather

Courage!

After a five-year struggle with rheumatic fever, a Houston boy was bewildered and pitifully weak. At age ten, Dan Rather had been housebound for months before having to spend most of a year flat on his back in bed. When his father carried him outside the house for the first time, he was bedeviled with inner questions.

Would he ever get over feeling like a caged animal? How long would it take him before he could again walk erect rather than be carried in his father's arms? What could he do to regain the weight he had lost? What did the doctor mean by saying he might have heart complications?

Pressing as they were, these issues took a backseat to his overwhelming distress. "I'd lost my sense of self," he later wrote. "I'd been like everybody else; now I was different."

In 1946 he did not know that in a variety of ways he would always be different. As a frightened boy of ten, he yearned to be like everyone else.

Years earlier, when he had started to earn money as a newsboy, he had looked and felt much like all the other newsboys of Houston. Because he was younger than many of his competitors, he had to scrap for his corner at Eighteenth Street and North Shepherd Drive. Other boys, sometimes bigger and older, tried to stop him from waving the Sunday *Chronicle* at passersby; they had corners of their own, but they didn't like the presence of a competitor nearby.

Dan, who was decidedly skinny, sometimes had to defend himself with his fists. Occasionally that meant he had a few bruises from his enterprise, but on a good Saturday evening he could pick up as much as three dollars, which was big money for a youngster from a run-of-the-mill community seven miles from downtown Houston.

Imitating his father, he had already adopted a mental slogan that slowly began to set him apart from other boys his age: COURAGE! (not simply "courage").

His father, Rather decided years later, must have repeated that same motto when he was having a rough time as an oil-line pipe layer. From the time Dan was lifted from his sickbed unable to walk, he found that COURAGE! helped to put him back on his feet. Throughout his life, as a rising reporter and news commentator, he used that motto to begin or to end his notes and occasionally made it his broadcast sign-off.

Rather needed all the courage he could muster when he enrolled at Sam Houston State College in Huntsville. Without financial assistance he could not stay in school, so he tried out for football because the school's players were given rent-free dormitory rooms. This time COURAGE! was not enough; he lacked the weight and sheer muscle power to perform well on the playing field.

Fortunately, a journalism professor, Hugh Cunningham, helped him find a part-time job at radio station KSAM— known as Kay Sam and often called "a teakettle." Rather became a jack of all broadcasting trades.

Operating on 250 watts, the three-room station's signal reached only a few miles. It paid the apprentice newscaster-sportscaster forty cents an hour with an occasional "talent fee" for broadcasting a football game. Rather covered everything from junior high school games to executions at the state prison.

Looking back on the job that became his "scholarship," Rather regarded his time there as an interval whose impact was much greater than its length. Kay Sam set him on the road to a career in mass media. Partly because it was "the kind of place where you could make a lot of mistakes," he learned a lot more than he realized at the time.

After graduation he taught journalism and worked successively for United Press International and the *Houston Chronicle* before taking a job at radio station KTRH in Houston. The station was affiliated with CBS, and it proved to be a stepping-stone to Houston's more prestigious KHOU-TV.

Long-time acquaintances smile when they say, "It took a hurricane to bring Dan a really big promotion." They are referring to Hurricane Carla, which approached the Texas coast along a very uncertain track in September 1961. Rather had a hard time persuading his colleagues and the station's decision makers that he should go to Galveston. Only there, he argued, was it possible to track the storm effectively—because Galveston's radar was the best in the state. Even though the nation's largest peacetime evacuation up to that time—350,000 persons—was under way, Rather received permission to move against the human tide.

Rather became the first person to send a radar scan of a hurricane to television viewers throughout the nation. While marooned on Galveston Island, one of his cameras captured the image of a frantic horse trying to escape from its pen. That brief shot spawned a story, still very much alive, that Rather calmly freed the terrified animal. The newsman disavows that he did any such thing.

Horse rescuer or not, his graphic coverage of the hurricane led to his promotion to head of CBS's southwestern bureau in Dallas. Two years later he directed the bureau's round-the-clock coverage of the John F. Kennedy assassination. Rather later said that he believed his accurate and impartial coverage of the traumatic event greatly contributed to the credibility of electronic journalism. This coverage also brought him to the attention of his network's executives.

Friends called him crazy when he turned down a promotion to New York. Ninety days later the network executives came back with a better offer, so the Houston native found himself in the nation's largest city on February 28, 1964. He had been there less than two years when he was made the network's White House correspondent.

Rather stayed in Washington only briefly before going to London as bureau chief and then to the killing fields of South Vietnam. Hampered by the fact that no one seemed to know the truth about anything, he found his assignment in Vietnam one of the most frustrating of his career. Seeing himself as there to report the news exactly as he saw it, his inability to get accurate news was a source of constant anxiety.

Back at the White House late in 1966, he regretfully concluded that the credibility gap between Texas native Lyndon B.

His disarming smile gives no hint that when convictions are involved, Dan Rather can be as hard as a deamond-tipped drill in a Texas oil field.

Johnson and the general public was growing. Years earlier Rather had met Johnson for the first time at the LBJ Ranch, where he was reprimanded for using a telephone without permission. In Washington, Rather said that the president sometimes "blowtorched" him, but Lady Bird was "beautiful to work with."

The credibility of the administration became a highly personal issue for Rather when a presidential secretary denied the validity of a report delivered on the air by Rather. Ten days later Secretary of Defense Robert S. McNamara confirmed the accuracy of Rather's initial report. Incidents such as this caused the reporter from Texas to feel that his White House beat was "journalistically as dangerous as routinely handling nitroglycerine."

In an era when few journalists dared antagonize the president, Rather politely but firmly tangled with Johnson regularly. The reporter's relations with the White House worsened in the next administration. Rather believed that Richard M. Nixon's spokesmen deliberately tried to mislead reporters. Both John

*Dan Rather knew the only
chief executive from Texas
intimately; the Lyndon B.
Johnson Library in Austin
holds the text of a very
long interview between the
reporter and the president.*

Ehrlichman and H. R. Haldeman branded some of Rather's
reports as "inaccurate and biased." Ehrlichman tried, without
success, to have him reassigned.

A confrontation between the reporter and the president
became a minor cause célèbre. Rather affronted President
Nixon at a meeting of the National Association of Broadcasters
in Houston at a session billed as an open press conference but
which Rather said was nothing of the sort. Trying to stem
rising indignation about the Watergate affair, administration
officials packed the hall with Republican faithfuls who would
cheer whatever Nixon said.

The president answered a few perfunctory questions, but
the burning issues were not addressed. With an estimated
three or four minutes of press conference time left, Rather
was recognized by the president. He felt some duress, certain that nothing substantive would come out of the session
and aware that he was at the top of Nixon's list of most
despised reporters.

President Richard M. Nixon misunderstood not only the actions and questions of Dan Rather but also the mood of Congress and the nation when the Watergate scandal began to unravel.

Rather was barely on his feet when the president questioned him: "Are you running for something, Mr. Rather?"

Rather's spur-of-the-moment response was, "No, sir, Mr. President. Are you?"

Still insisting that he did not mean to insult or even challenge the chief executive, Rather does admit that he made a mistake. Yet as a journalist, he contends, "In our system, no citizen has to face any leader on bended knee."

Many of his colleagues in the press were shocked or outraged by his response to Nixon's taunt. Angry viewers wrote letters denouncing Rather's conduct, and some CBS affiliates demanded his resignation. He not only weathered the storm that hit Houston that night, Rather was one of the contributing correspondents who made CBS's *60 Minutes* one of the most widely watched and respected television documentary programs. Guiding *CBS Reports,* he won the respect of his peers. Later he succeeded Walter Cronkite as anchor of *CBS Evening News* and guided *Forty-eight Hours* to international fame.

When he published his personal account of the Watergate era under the title of *The Palace Guard,* it was the first of his several best-selling books. These recollections helped him to maintain his place as one of the most respected analysts to share his views through the medium of television.

20

San Jacinto

Sixteen Minutes to Independence

One jubilant soldier in Sam Houston's little army said that he had looked at his pocket watch as the opening gun was fired at San Jacinto. According to him, the battle that won independence for Texas lasted "maybe a hair over sixteen minutes."

Some of his comrades disagreed. They claimed that only fifteen minutes had passed before the last Mexican soldier was on the ground, in the water, or taking to his heels.

Events had moved swiftly in the weeks preceding one of the shortest decisive battles in North American annals. On March 2, 1836, Texas leaders issued a declaration of independence, David G. Burnet was made head of the provisional government, and Sam Houston's appointment as commander of Texas armed forces was confirmed.

Less than two weeks later, Texas forces under James G. Fannin were captured and executed by Gen. José Urrea's army. On March 17, the delegates who were assembled at Washington-on-the-Brazos adopted a constitution formally organizing a new and independent government.

Houston, who had no formal military training and limited experience in combat, earlier had decided that his army could not face Gen. Antonio López de Santa Anna's army on equal terms. He realized that his shortage of field artillery made his forces vulnerable. Stephen F. Austin was sent to search for more cannon but had no luck. As a result, by the time Houston expected to face Santa Anna, the Texas commander in chief had only two small guns, popularly known as the Twin Sisters.

Knowing that he was badly outnumbered and outgunned, Houston conserved his men and ammunition by staging a series of defensive retreats for more than month. To his credit, volunteers joined his army nonetheless. Word of the Alamo and Goliad massacres had terrified the great mass of colonists but also emboldened some to fight. On April 18 Houston camped near Harrisburg in present-day Harris County.

The Texans were tired of constantly moving to elude capture, and they wanted the opportunity to fight. Their leader flashed a grim smile when he read a dispatch taken from a Mexican prisoner. If the document was accurate, the odds in favor of the enemy had changed considerably. No longer outnumbered three or four to one, Houston's force of around 750 men now seemed only slightly smaller than the 1,000 Mexicans who were reported to be headed toward the San Jacinto River.

On April 20, after two days of hard marching, the Texans made contact with a unit of Mexican cavalry. Knowing the Brazos River to be at flood stage, Houston tried to maneuver his opponents into a corner from which they could not emerge without a fight. By seizing the only functional ferry within miles, he believed he could accomplish his goal. In a hasty note dispatched to a longtime friend, Houston wrote of the impending battle: "It is the only chance of saving Texas. Wisdom and necessity say that we must meet the enemy now. The troops are in fine spirits, and now is the time for action."

Santa Anna was not unaware of Houston's presence. His scouts reported on the size of the Texas force, and the Mexican commander decided on a prudent course. Sending a messenger for reinforcements under Gen. Martin Perfecto Cos, whose troops were a hard day's march away, he directed his own troops to camp close to the river and throw up defensive works.

Massachusetts-born Sidney Sherman of Kentucky did not like the idea of spending the night without striking at the foe, so he led a band of fifty riders against the Mexican pickets. His force, which included Mirabeau B. Lamar, stirred up a general alarm but had no other effect.

An early depiction of the battle of San Jacinto offers a view of an assault against a strongly entrenched position—somewhat unlike the actual clash in a bayou.

Squatting by a campfire, Houston concluded that Santa Anna would launch a full-scale attack the next day. Thus the Tennessee native decided it would be better for him to strike the first blow. Houston did not know that Cos was goading his men so fiercely that he would lead more than 500 of them into the Mexican camp before first light. The reinforcements would give Santa Anna more than 1,500 men on the field of battle.

Houston entrusted a veteran scout with a special mission. For communication, Erastus Smith was dependent upon lipreading and hand signals, and he was known to his comrades as "Deaf Smith." Nevertheless, he followed orders to destroy the bridge over the San Jacinto River, preventing the Mexicans from avoiding the fight.

Unable to sleep, Houston was in the saddle soon after midnight. Under his direction, the Texans slowly and cautiously moved their two fieldpieces within range of the Mexican barricades. Texas riders fanned out with orders to contain Santa Anna's cavalry, regardless of what it might take. Moving slowly to make as little noise as possible, Houston's tiny band of infantry formed a single column.

At noon the Texans held a war council. Houston announced that he planned to attack on the morning of April 22, and his officers agreed. The lower ranks, however, were impatient and rebellious. Each company took a vote and overwhelming announced that they wanted to fight immediately. Houston agreed, knowing now that his men were angry enough to fight and determined to fight.

The Mexican army, meanwhile, had expected that the Texans would attack that morning. When noon passed, Santa Anna decided that the Texans were waiting for the next day. He decided to rest his men. Further complicating the Mexican situation was the fact that for two months Santa Anna had moved at will through Texas, crushing any opposition with little effort, notwithstanding the delay at the Alamo. This sense of invulnerability mixed with the humid April warmth to generate overconfidence. The Mexican army relaxed.

The Texans formed into a line that spread across a thousand yards. They were armed with rifles, bowie knives, and tomahawks. A thousand men stood on the verge of a thousand legends. They looked to the center, where Houston sat mounted next to their makeshift flag. On their flanks were the black waters of the bayou.

Spurring his horse into sudden movement, Houston reached the head of his column and gave a signal. Gunners responded by firing both cannon simultaneously. A quartet of musicians was ignorant of any martial music but well versed in the popular music of the day. They began playing a popular tune called "Come to the Bower," which some regarded as risque.

Tired, hungry, and angry, the army leveled its weapons and began to move across the plain. They marched across the grasslands, up a swell, and into the Mexican camp. Santa Anna had not posted any pickets and had not sent any scouts to watch the Texas camps. The sound of the Mexican bugles were muted by shouts of "Remember the Alamo!" and "Remember Goliad!" The Texans fired a volley at a distance of less than sixty yards.

At midafternoon the Texas army of almost one thousand men marched across a mile of open grassland on a bright, sunny day and took a veteran force of at least twelve hundred men by surprise. Many Mexicans did not even pick up their

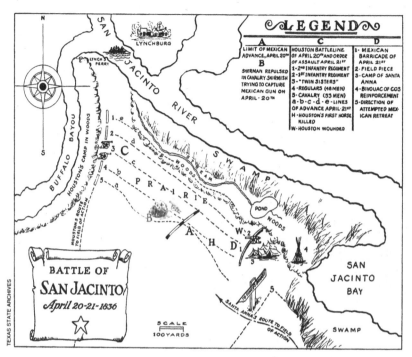

The battle of San Jacinto put the Mexican army at a disadvantage because it was backed up to water and swamp.

weapons; instead they bolted to the rear, momentarily forgetting that they were running toward deep water. Their only cannon was fired hastily. Its grapeshot flew high over the Texans' heads.

The surging line swept the barricades. The Mexicans could not form their lines, reload their weapons, or wield their bayonets. Like most European armies of the time, they were trained to fight in a disciplined manner, not as individuals. The Texans ran through them with rifle butts and long-bladed knives.

Within fifteen minutes after the first shot was fired, Gen. Manuel Castrillon and a dozen other Mexican officers were casualties. Many, perhaps hundreds, of their men became mired in swamps or drowned in the river or in nearby Buffalo Bayou. Houston had lost two horses in the attack and been wounded in the ankle. His orders for the army to reform went

Sam Houston was elected the first president of the Republic of Texas largely for the role he played in defeating the Mexican army at San Jacinto.

unheeded as the Texans sought revenge for the eight hundred men of the Alamo and Goliad.

That evening, Houston sat propped up against a tree as reports were made. Two Texans had been killed and thirty had been wounded, but seven of these would die. Six hundred Mexicans lay on the field, and as many or more had been captured, including Santa Anna. Only Houston's intercession prevented the Mexican president-general from being shot. With him in their possession, the Texans were free to dictate their terms for independence. The battle for Texas had been won.

This short combat between forces so small that San Jacinto barely qualifies as a battle brought independence to Texas, yet measured by its results, it was one of the most decisive battles of history. The freedom won here led to annexation and the Mexican War, which resulted in the United States gaining nearly one million square miles of territory—today's states of Texas, New Mexico, Arizona, Nevada, California, Utah, and parts of Colorado, Wyoming, Kansas, and Oklahoma. Houston was elected president of the new republic early in the fall of 1836, and a few months later the United States recognized it as a nation despite Mexico's refusal to relinquish its claims.

21
Valverde, New Mexico
Iron Hail

Born in Gallatin, Tennessee, William R. Scurry moved to San Antonio at the age of sixteen and offered his services to his adopted state as soon as war broke out between the North and the South. By the time a Confederate force met the Federal army at Valverde in the New Mexico Territory, Scurry was a lieutenant colonel of the Fourth Regiment of Texas Mounted Volunteers. Describing the desperate charge that decided the day, the young man wrote:

> Just before sunset Lieut. Thomas P. Ochiltree brought an order to prepare for a charge all along the line. All prepared for its prompt execution, and when the words "Up boys, and at them!" were given, straight at their battery of six guns, supported by columns of infantry and cavalry, some 700 yards in front of our position, went our brave volunteers, unmindful of the driving storm of grape and canister and musket balls sent hurling around them. With yells and ringing shouts they dashed on, until the guns were won and the enemy in full retreat before them.

Scurry, who became a brigadier general seven months later, said little about his role in the battle. According to Capt. T. T. Teel, however, during fierce hand-to-hand fighting the voice of the Tennessee native could be heard "above the din of battle and smoke, and flame, and death, encouraging the men to stand by their posts."

Brig. Gen. H. H. Sibley was responsible for the violent clash on the upper Rio Grande. Late in 1861 he conceived a plan to

135

drive the Federals from the New Mexico Territory so that it could be annexed by the Confederacy. Advancing deep into the region, he then turned south in a move interpreted by his foes as a retreat. Soon it was apparent that he was not headed back to Texas; rather, he hoped to take isolated Fort Craig.

With buildings protected by "sand-revetted mud walls," the garrison was vital to controlling the surrounding region. Confederate Lt. Col. John R. Baylor of the Mounted Rifles had come within sight of the fortress in August 1861. Had his horses not been jaded, he reported, he could easily have taken it.

Five months later, Sibley and his twenty-six hundred men moved toward Fort Craig despite difficulties. His soldiers, he wrote, were "poorly armed, thinly clad, and almost destitute of blankets." To make things worse, smallpox and pneumonia had stricken his force. Always cautious, Sibley sent a scouting party ahead when he came within a day's march of the little fortress.

Reconnaissance indicated that light fieldpieces could not level the Federal defenses. Hence Sibley decided to force the enemy into "an open-field fight" at a ford about six miles down the river. Thirsty Confederates whose horses had not been watered for twenty-four hours whooped with delight upon reaching the Rio Grande. Camped near it on February 20, they lost one hundred and perhaps more than two hundred still-thirsty mules that stampeded and fell into Union hands. Since he no longer had the animals to pull them, Sibley burned most of his wagons. That meant he must either win a victory against great odds or move toward Texas without supplies and ammunition.

Fighting began early on the morning of February 21, and by 10:00 A.M. fire from six pieces commanded by Union Capt. Alexander McRae had cut big holes in the Confederate lines. Maj. Henry W. Ragnet of the Fourth Texas Cavalry replied to the Federal fire as best he could with a single light gun that was soon hit and partly disabled.

All horses used to pull Ragnet's piece were killed by noon. In desperation he called for volunteers to move it by hand. Though subjected to what he called "the hottest cannonading on that part of the field," his men somehow recovered the gun. They then turned it upon the enemy whose two 24-pound howitzers were beginning to hit their targets.

A charge was ordered. About one thousand men stepped from behind the low sand hills and entered a level area with

The 1862 battle of Valverde was a dramatic Southern victory borne by shotguns and revolvers against well-equipped Union troops.

no cover except an occasional sapling. At a signal, they divided into two columns and raced toward Federal fieldpieces and howitzers. "For the first time, perhaps, on record," Sibley reported, "batteries were charged and taken at the muzzle of double-barreled shot-guns, thus illustrating the spirit, valor, and invincible determination of Texas troops. Nobly have they emulated the fame of their San Jacinto ancestors."

Sibley's exultation was warranted. Brig. Gen. Edward R. S. Canby not only had more and bigger guns than did his foe, he commanded a force of thirty-eight hundred men that included volunteers from New Mexico and Colorado. Col. Christopher Carson, later famous as Kit, led a regiment that included eight companies. Sibley had only twenty-six hundred men, but some were veterans of the Mexican War.

Most units, both Confederate and Federal, were forced to cross the river two or three times during the twenty-four hours of fighting. Many Union volunteers balked, refusing to go through swift water that was waist deep above quicksand. Under fire, these men were so demoralized that about one hundred of them deserted in a body, cutting the Federal manpower margin to eleven hundred.

Though their afternoon charge won the day, the Confederates were not entirely successful. A company of about forty lancers, led by Capt. Willis L. Lang, made a gallant but futile

Gen. Edward R. S. Canby was lauded in Montgomery and Richmond for his "brilliant strategy" at Valverde.

LESLIE'S ILLUSTRATED HISTORY OF THE CIVIL WAR

assault. His little unit of lightly armed men was described in official reports as having been decimated. Lt. D. M. Bass, a survivor, sustained seven wounds.

Capt. W. P. Hardeman of the Fourth Texas Mounted Volunteers was the hero of the day. According to the pro-Union *Sante Fe Gazette,* Hardeman's charge was "without a parallel in the history of ancient or modern warfare." He and his men, said the newspaper, "advanced steadily on foot, armed principally with Colt's six-shooters. The iron hail through which they passed cut through their ranks, making in them frightful vacancies, but it had no other effect."

Like Scurry, Hardeman was a Tennessean who had reached Texas in 1835. During the New Mexico campaign he saw as many men die of exhaustion as were killed by Federal bullets. Late in December 1864, Jefferson Davis requested Confederate lawmakers to make him a brigadier.

All but forgotten today, Valverde is ranked by some military historians as one of the most dramatic battles of the Civil War. An inferior Confederate force whose raw courage was supported largely by shotguns and revolvers routed a body that included more than one-tenth of all effective soldiers in the U.S. Army.

Part 5
A Matter of Timing

The difference of a few hours in February 1861 might have seen Robert E. Lee as a prisoner of the Texas militia rather than in command of Virginia's troops early in the war.

22
Robert E. Lee
By the Skin of His Teeth

Old-timers in Austin, Galveston, and San Antonio disagreed over many matters, but in late January 1861 they were practically unanimous about one thing: The turmoil among Texans was practically at the same fever-pitch as it was on the eve of the Texas Revolution. Nine out of ten Texans took it for granted that trouble was brewing between the former independent republic and the Washington government.

South Carolina had started the secession ball rolling, and it was assumed that Texas would soon be among the former states. Of course, like the other seceded states, there were several Federal installations scattered across the state and a significant number of Unionists.

When the legislature convened on January 21, Gov. Sam Houston urged caution but consented to a statewide vote. The referendum came much sooner than Houston expected. On February 1, a special convention passed an ordinance of secession. The language of the document was adapted largely from that framed in South Carolina on December 20, 1860.

With no one knowing how many Federal soldiers were in the state, primarily to protect settlers from Indians, many Texans realized they might soon need money for weapons and equipment. Houston was authorized to float a one-hundred-thousand-dollar loan to equip a small army.

A Committee of Public Safety, already in existence, suddenly loomed to new importance. Because distances were great and travel was slow, committee members decided to establish not one but three military forces. Ben McCulloch was

141

authorized to recruit men in and around San Antonio, Henry E. McCulloch was placed in charge of recruitment in the northwestern frontier, and John S. Ford was assigned to the lower Rio Grande. All three men knew that a few hundred amateurs did not have much chance for success against a large body of trained professional soldiers.

At his headquarters in San Antonio, Gen. David Twiggs was distraught. He had repeatedly petitioned the War Department to be relieved of command. In response to the secession crisis, he had announced that he was not willing to fire on fellow Americans under any circumstances.

On February 15, Twiggs found relief—of a sort. McCulloch marched into San Antonio that morning at the head of a thousand volunteer soldiers. As they proceeded toward Twiggs's headquarters, they were joined by at least one hundred townspeople. The arsenal buildings and a commissary were surrounded before first light, and riflemen were stationed strategically. McCulloch sent Twiggs a written demand for "the surrender of all public property and post." Twiggs, who had already chosen to join the Secessionists, bowed to the ultimatum and drafted a dispatch that ordered the evacuation of all army posts in Texas.

A little over two weeks later, on March 2, the public referendum withdrew the state from the Union. Texas was once more "a free and independent sovereignty."

AT FORT MASON, a five-day ride north of San Antonio, the U.S. Army's Second Cavalry realized that news was always stale when it reached the base. Its commander chafed because momentous events were taking place too far away to be tracked. He had been with his men only a few weeks after an absence of more than two years; now he might soon be caught up in changes that could lead to permanent separation from his veteran riders.

Wondering about the course of events over which he had no control, Robert E. Lee almost certainly reflected at length about his own career. The fifth child of "Light Horse Harry" Lee of Revolutionary War fame, Robert had won appointment to West Point and graduated second in the forty-six-man class of 1829.

His high academic standing allowed his placement in the corps of engineers. In that role the second lieutenant was assigned to duty at several forts under construction and then at St. Louis. He saw no combat until the outbreak of the Mexican War. During the first U.S. "foreign war," Lee won the lasting friendship of Gen. Winfield Scott—later a candidate for the presidency and general in chief of all U.S. armed forces.

Back in the states, the Virginian became superintendent of the U.S. Military Academy at West Point. At a time when Lee might have anticipated a posting to Washington, the secretary of war, Jefferson Davis, included Lee among the hand-picked officers for the elite First and Second Cavalries. Lee was sent to West Texas as the Second Cavalry's second in command, serving under Albert Sydney Johnston. Arriving at his post in 1857, he was frequently given court-martial duty and other affairs.

He sought a leave of absence when his father-in-law died and left his estate, Arlington, as well as its debts to Lee's wife. Lee labored for two years to pay off the accumulated debts and restore some of the lost luster to Arlington. He pondered his future in the military, weighing that against retirement. Promotion was slow. There was the possibility that his path had been blocked by officers jealous of Lee's relationship with Scott. Was he "tainted" in the eyes of general staff because his wife was a descendant of Martha Washington and had come into possession of Arlington?

Lee was at Arlington in 1859 when news of John Brown's raid on Harpers Ferry reached Washington. Since he was the highest ranking line officer in the area, Lee was ordered to lead the only troops in the capital, a contingent of U.S. Marines at the Washington Naval Yard, to deal with Brown. Jeb Stuart, a young cavalry lieutenant, was in Washington with a proposal regarding standard horse soldier equipment and was ordered to join the force as Lee's aide. Shortly after arriving in Harpers Ferry, the marines stormed Brown's sanctuary and seized him. Lee's performance there made him a hero to the South, but many in the North despised him as "a defender of slave owners."

In late 1860 he returned to his Second Cavalry post in Texas. What he found was not the disciplined command he had left

Lt. Col. R. E. Lee had fought at Cerro Gordo and Chapultec in the Mexican War and served as commandant of cadets at West Point before being assigned to the elite Second Cavalry in Texas.

NEW YORK PUBLIC LIBRARY

but a chaotic situation caught up in the Secessionist crisis. Many officers from the South were contemplating resigning their commissions should the Union dissolve. As an officer in the federal army, Lee recognized his allegiance was to the Union as long as Virginia was still a part of that Union. His anxiety about the course Texas would take was relieved when he received orders to report personally to Winfield Scott in Washington.

He packed his gear hurriedly, knowing he might never return to Texas. His ambulance—a vehicle typically used by officers for long trips—was ready on the evening of February 12. Promotion would hardly call for a visit to the general in chief. Did Scott have a position in Washington in mind? That seemed improbable.

As the former commandant of Fort Mason seated himself in the ambulance, Lt. R. W. Johnson ran to the vehicle and asked, "Colonel, which way will you go—North, or South?"

Lee responded without hesitation: "I shall never bear arms against the Union—but circumstances may force me to carry a musket in defense of Virginia."

Mary Lee, a descendant of Martha Washington, became the owner of Arlington mansion when her father, George Washington Parke Custis, died in 1857. He left the estate heavily in debt. The restoration of the property and payment of the debts was left to her husband, Robert E. Lee, which he accomplished by 1859.

DICTIONARY OF AMERICAN PORTRAITS

He reached San Antonio's Read House early on the afternoon of February 16. He was soon surrounded by a crowd curious to hear what an army officer might have to say. He was surprised to learn of the coup staged by McCulloch and his men a few hours before his arrival. McCulloch's men had escorted several army personnel out of town and made prisoners of some. A small number of soldiers staged a daring escape to Mexico, but several of them were captured and detained—some for days, weeks, or months. Some spent two years in stockades and prisons.

Had Lee reached San Antonio a few hours later, he might have been arrested by the Texas militia. Warily, he dressed in civilian clothes. He then headed for Indianola in hope of finding a steamer that would take him to New Orleans.

One of his former officers, Lt. R. M. Potter, came to bid him good-bye and saw that Lee was distraught. According to Potter, Lee said that he did not believe secession was a constitutional right but feared that Virginia might secede. "When I get back to the Old Dominion," Lee told Potter, "the country is likely to have one soldier less; I think I may resign and go to planting corn." During the two weeks it took Lee to reach New Orleans and catch a train for Alexandria, Virginia, Lee heard nothing from Texas.

THROUGHOUT FEBRUARY and March 1861, the U.S. Army slowly pulled out of Texas, relinquishing forts and equipment to the Texas militia. Reflecting upon these swift changes, Col. C. A. Waite of the First U.S. Infantry noted: "The moment the secession movement commenced, the people of Texas became much excited on that subject, and immediately after the passage of the secession ordinance, several large bodies of Texans were collected and threatened an attack upon some of our posts. There is a strong feeling against the Central Government, and the Army, being the representative of its power, shares that dislike."

Waite succeeded Twiggs in command of the Department of Texas, and he was convinced that "the first blood shed would be a prelude to a general attack on the [2,684 members of the U.S.] Army" then in the state.

Before Lee reached Alexandria, Camps Cooper and Colorado were formally abandoned, and Secessionists seized U.S. property at Brazos Santiago. Throughout the month of March 1861 Federal outposts were abandoned, including Lee's former command at Fort Mason. Across the state, the militia moved to capture as many Federal soldiers as possible.

In the nation's capital, Lee met with General Scott, but no record was made of their conversation. Promoted to full colonel, Lee met with Francis P. Blair, one of the inner circle of advisers to President Abraham Lincoln, whose task was "to ascertain the feelings and intentions" of Colonel Lee. Although no record was made of their conversation, it is believed that Lee was offered field command of the U.S. Army, which he declined.

The next day, though grateful for his promotion, Lee submitted his resignation to Scott. The aged general in chief accepted it but sadly pronounced, "Lee, you have made the greatest mistake of your life, but I feared it would be so." The two men never saw each other again.

U.S. Marines under Robert E. Lee killed or captured everyone who had been led to Harpers Ferry, Virginia, by abolitionist John Brown.

A few days later Lee attended services at Christ Church, then received a letter urging him immediately to go to the Virginia capital to meet with Gov. John Letcher. He had no idea what Letcher expected of him, but he was also keenly aware that there were several Federal installations in Virginia, much as there had been in Texas. In Texas numerous army officers were under arrest and others had sworn a formal pledge, or parole, not to fight before December 1862. Had Lee been among those captured, he might have been unable to don a

Confederate uniform until the spring of 1863—and the fortunes of war might have been remarkably different.

Lee was barely able to get out of Texas without being arrested and imprisoned. Had weather or horses caused his schedule to change by a single day, the story of the Civil War and hence that of the nation might have been quite different.

23
Sabine Pass

Victory or Death!

Occupied by Federal troops, New Orleans was in a state of excitement on the morning of September 4, 1863. Afterward, Lt. Henry C. Dane of the U.S. Signal Service informed *New York Herald* readers of what was afoot: "A large expedition was leaving on some unrevealed, but avowedly very important mission. The levee was crowded with men, women, and children, where troops were embarking and transports were moving away down the Mississippi river, among grim and sullen-looking men-of-war."

Four days later, Dane wrote, a council of war was held aboard an ironclad. When it ended, "The large fleet of transports, attended by six gunboats, were now ready to assault, capture and possess the southern half of the great State of Texas."

A successful expedition would cut off the flow of Texas cotton to England and Europe. Equally important to the Union, a Federal victory would discourage France from seizing control of Mexico. If such a base were established, U.S. officials feared the next step would be a European invasion from the southwest.

With tiny Fort Grigsby their objective, twenty-seven vessels collected by Rear Adm. David G. Farragut set out for the Sabine River. Long a boundary between the United States and Mexico, the stream flowed through a lake close to the gulf. Only seven miles long below the lake, the Sabine was usually nearly a mile across with wide mud flats on each side. Near its mouth an oyster bed three hundred yards wide stretched for about a mile. Although this natural obstacle divided the river into two channels, intelligence reports claimed that its average depth of twenty to forty feet was more than adequate for vessels of light draft.

Whooping with enthusiasm, approximately 6,000 soldiers and sailors crowded on deck to wave good-bye to New Orleans. Already 180 of their best marksmen had been selected to serve as sharpshooters for the expedition commanded by Brig. Gen. William B. Franklin.

For the council of war aboard the 197-ton USS *Sachem,* Franklin called together Gens. Godfrey Weitzel and William Emory and Lt. Frederick Crocker, who headed the naval phase of the joint operation. According to Dane's report, it was decided to send two gunboats up the river to draw the fire of Confederate Fort Griffin. Weitzel would head 500 picked men who would land on the Texas shore to storm the fort from the rear.

About the time the Federal battle plans were being drawn up, Confederate Lt. Richard Dowling called his men to attention. Named the Davis Guard, in honor of Jefferson Davis, members of the unit were popularly known as the Dockwallopers. Now they constituted Company F, First Regiment, Texas Heavy Artillery.

The twenty-five-year-old Dowling reported that a Federal force of overpowering strength was believed to be headed toward their fort. Brig. Gen. John B. Magruder, who had sent the news, suggested an orderly withdrawal. Unwilling to take this course, Dowling announced that he would stay, but anyone who wished to leave could do so. Astonished by the offer, the forty men glanced at one another, whispered, and then shouted in unison, "Victory or death!"

The mud walls of the tiny installation made seasoned fighting men wonder how it came to be called a fort. Yet inside were crowded two 32-pounders, two 24-pounders, and two brass-mounted howitzers. With 180 charges of powder hastily secured from the nearby town of Sabine, the men inside Fort Griffin prepared for action. Sand was removed to lower the front of one of their biggest guns so it could fire downward toward the river.

Weeks earlier, members of the garrison had practiced with their artillery and placed distance markers at the river's edge. When assistant surgeon George H. Bailey arrived and offered

THE SOLDIER IN OUR CIVIL WAR

Federal gunboats converged in preparation for the attack upon Sabine Pass.

to help, he was assigned to one of the guns. Dowling took charge of a two-gun section that included "Annie," named for his wife. Once the hasty preparations were completed, there was nothing to do but watch and wait.

Around 6:30 A.M. on September 8 the 892-ton USS *Clifton* moved into the west, or Texas, channel and opened fire on the fort. During the first hour twenty-six shells were fired from its 32-pounders, 9-inch Dahlgren guns, and 30-pounder Parrott rifles. Two shots hit the mud installation but did little damage. To the surprise of the attackers, no response came from Fort Griffin.

After the *Clifton* withdrew, all was quiet until the tiny CSS *Uncle Ben* steamed downriver. Armed with only two

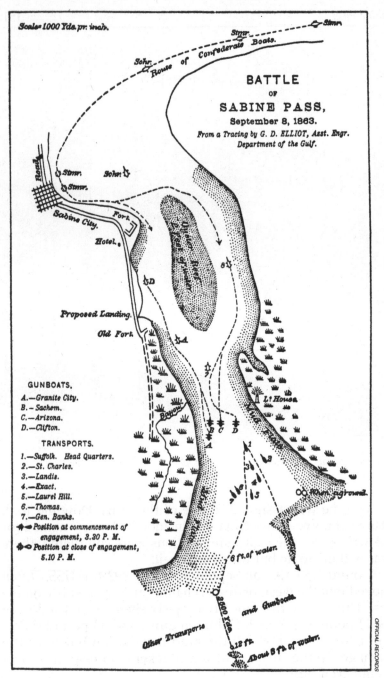

The battle of Sabine Pass could not have gone better for the Confederate defenders. Prior to the engagement they had tagged the river with range markers. The effective fire from the Southern batteries disabled or repelled every Union ship that approached.

The Union gunboat Sachem *was among those disabled in the attack upon Sabine Pass.*

12-pounders, the Confederate vessel was known as a cotton-clad because bales of cotton rather than sheets of iron constituted its protective armor.

When the *Uncle Ben* came within range, gunners aboard the USS *Sachem* fired their 30-pounder Parrott rifle three times without effect. All Federal vessels then pulled out of range until a concerted action began at 3:40 P.M.

Both the *Sachem* and the 959-ton USS *Arizona* moved up the east, or Louisiana, channel while the *Clifton* remained poised to use the west channel. When the ironclads were twelve hundred yards from the fort, Dowling opened fire with his entire battery. Minutes later a ball passed through the boiler of the *Sachem* and a white flag was hoisted as a signal of surrender to the tiny *Uncle Ben*.

By this time the *Clifton*'s big guns were within easy range of their target. A well-placed shot from shore carried away the

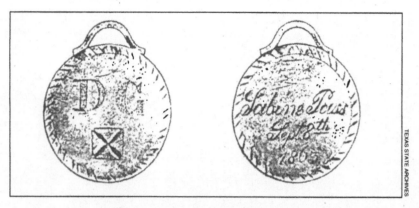

TEXAS STATE ARCHIVES

The Davis Guard Medal, inexpertly carved from Mexican silver dollars, was one of the very few medals conferred upon Confederate soldiers.

vessel's tiller rope, so the *Clifton* floundered about, eventually grounding in the mud about five hundred yards from the fort. Sharpshooters crowded the deck and maintained a heavy fire for twenty-five minutes, after which another white flag went up.

The limited navigable water and the Confederate distance markers proved too much for the overwhelmingly superior Federal firepower. After just thirty-eight minutes, the invasion of Texas was halted and the vessels still able to retire did so as quickly as possible.

Some aboard the *Sachem* were scalded when the ship's boiler was hit. So many men jumped from their vessels and were drowned that the Federal death toll reached 56. Crocker and about 350 others were taken prisoner. Reporting on the results, Dowling estimated the two captured gunboats to be worth one million dollars. He stressed that not a man in the fort had been lost.

After the defeat, Maj. Gen. Nathaniel P. Banks, commander of the Department of the Gulf, reported the failure of the invasion directly to the president. The failure, he insisted, stemmed from "the insufficient naval force with which the attempt was made." In turn, Lieutenant Crocker's naval report placed the blame on the army.

A formal court of inquiry, directed primarily at the conduct aboard the transports *Arizona* and *Granite City*, concluded that a court-martial was warranted but not recommended. Meanwhile, all plans for the conquest of Texas were set aside.

The reaction in Richmond, naturally, was quite different. A formal resolution of thanks to the Davis Guards was voted by the Confederate Congress. President Davis praised their actions as among the most notable in the annals of warfare— mistakenly reporting the Federal force as having numbered ten thousand troops plus officers and seamen. In Texas, artisans filed Mexican silver dollars smooth, stamped them with the initials D.G. and presented Dowling and each of his men with one of the rarest Civil War medals.

A monument erected years later is inscribed with such names as Fitzgerald, Corcoran, Dougherty, Sullivan, McGrath, Monohan, and O'Hara. Most if not all the Davis Guards were feisty Irish Americans who defeated a Federal force at least 225 times as large as their own.

24
Mirabeau Buonaparte Lamar
Turn Around

"Fellow citizens . . ." No public speaker, Stephen F. Austin paused and started over: "Fellow citizens, we face a new day. I hope you will cast your votes for a new leader. Good ole Beau Lamar is no toady of Sam's. If he wins, things will be different."

A handful of Texans listening to Austin's stump speech in 1838 were well aware that he despised Sam Houston. According to Austin and others, the first president of the Republic of Texas, whose two-year term was soon ending, was nothing but "a tool of Andy Jackson."

Austin had been trounced at the polls in September 1836. With nearly six thousand ballots cast, the man who brought the first three hundred American settlers into the region received little more than a thousand votes. That was enough to make any man with backbone hold a grudge, the citizens reasoned. If Mirabeau Buonaparte Lamar was good enough to be Sam Houston's vice president, maybe he was good enough to fill the top office—in spite of his hifalutin name.

Politics aside, Lamar had been at the head of the Texas cavalry at the battle of San Jacinto. He had led the charge that broke the last shred of Mexican resistance. When he was promoted to a major general of the Texas army, Houston praised him for his action against Gen. Antonio López de Santa Anna's troops. Later Houston said that Lamar's performance in battle was the sole basis upon which he was made vice president of the republic in 1836.

Houston, who had begun taunting Lamar by calling him "the talented amateur," was very much aware that he was

156

poles apart in his outlook from his vice president. "Anybody but Beau," he repeatedly urged the voters. With the campaign for the presidency barely under way, matters became confused when Lamar's opponent committed suicide. The chief justice of Texas then stepped into the vacant slot, but within weeks he disappeared in Galveston Bay and was never seen again. Robert Wilson, a state senator who became the vice president's third opponent, received only 252 votes to Lamar's 6,995 votes.

Thus Lamar became the second president of the Republic of Texas and immediately surprised his fellow citizens by announcing how fortunate Texans were that the United States had chosen not to annex the Lone Star Republic. "It gives us a free hand," he explained, "and I will use it."

Soon the new chief executive was busy trying to win diplomatic recognition from England, the Netherlands, and France. Since Mexico refused to acknowledge the independence of its former state, Lamar contended that any foreign recognition would be in Texas's best interest.

It did not take long after the election for men with a little savvy to realize that they had put into power a man who was determined to reverse everything Sam Houston had achieved. Instead of consolidating those assets that Texas had, Lamar was determined to expand. The new republic, he said repeatedly, should include all land north and east of the Rio Grande.

The chief executive knew perfectly well that such a claim involved a lot of territory under Indian control. As a start toward making the expansion he wanted, it would be necessary to rid the republic of Houston's friends, the Cherokees. These people, said Lamar, were allies of the Mexicans; otherwise they would not have so many muskets.

The president sent Albert Sidney Johnston and two other commissioners to deal with the situation, by which he meant that tribes were ordered off land they had occupied for generations. Their chief, known to the Texans as Colonel Bowles, resisted. In a two-day battle that began on July 15, 1839, Bowles and many other Cherokees died and the fleeing survivors were pursued for ten days until most of them were killed.

Once these tribes were disposed of, Lamar's soldiers turned successively to smaller bands—Caddos, Shawnees, Delawares, Kickapoos, Creeks, and Muscogees. By the time the Seminoles

Mirabeau Lamar, like most early leaders of Texas, had fought in the revolution. They were not all like-minded politically, thus Lamar's differences with Sam Houston over U.S. annexation colored the scene for almost a decade.

became targets, their leaders knew that it would be hopeless to fight. Hence many of them volunteered to serve as scouts for the Texans.

The Comanches, however, were another story. Most of their territory was at a considerable distance from the Texan settlements, and they had no intention of giving up without a struggle. In January 1840 three chieftains rode into San Antonio and requested a hearing. Texas Ranger Henry W. Karnes reported to the secretary of war, Albert Sidney Johnston, that he treated them with courtesy and invited them to bring in their people—along with any whites being held as captives.

Numerous Comanche leaders with their families and captive Matilda Lockhart rode into San Antonio in March. Mukwar-rah, a medicine man, balked at being interrogated, and a fight ensued. Before it was over, about three dozen warriors were dead and another two dozen had surrendered.

The Rangers sent one of the Indian women to tell her people that Matilda said other whites were being held prisoner. She was instructed to tell her people that all the whites were to be freed or the Rangers would come and take them by force.

Nothing was heard from the messenger afterward, but Comanches soon descended in strength on the village of Linnville. This violent raid proved a prelude to forty years of constant warfare between the Texans and the Comanches, which ended only after Chief Quanah Parker led the remnants of his tribe to Fort Sill, Oklahoma.

Lamar instituted a series of internal improvements, but these proceeded along almost as rocky a road as the expulsion of the Indians. In the fall of 1839, Lamar sent five men to find a suitable spot for a permanent capital. Columbia, the temporary capital under Houston's administration, was considered by Lamar to be "wholly unsuited to house the government."

Lamar's men picked the village of Waterloo, on the north bank of the Colorado River. Against strong opposition from Houston, the president prevailed and the legislature confirmed the selection in 1840, changing the name of the new capital of the republic to Austin. At its incorporation late in 1839, Austin had nearly one thousand residents, some of whom helped to erect a one-story frame building designed to house the government office.

After his rise to political power, Houston went on record as believing Austin was "indefensible against Indians or Mexicans." This verdict was accurate since the town on the banks of the Colorado River lay well beyond the frontier of settlements. Security considerations prompted removal of the capital from Austin to Washington-on-the Brazos and later to Houston.

These moves, which appeared sensible to outsiders, did not suit Austin's handful of citizens. Personnel and what furniture the state owned were moved without incident. When Houston set out to transport the state archives to a new seat of government, however, the town became the center of a political firestorm known as "the Archives War."

Late in December 1842, wagons reached the Land Office, the repository of most state records. Before the drivers could begin to load their vehicles, irate citizens assembled and managed to aim a cannon at the Land Office. Tradition says that a woman fired the weapon, but even though the shot hit the

Sam Houston had tried to consolidate what Texas had won from Mexico, but Lamar was of a more expansionist mind-set.

building, it did little damage. During the ensuing turmoil, the all-important records were hastily dumped into the wagons, which were driven away with all speed.

The successful exit from Austin with the records should have put an end to the fracas, but it did not. Citizens of the capital formed a posse of sorts and set out in pursuit of the wagons, which they found parked for the night about three hours away from the town. Angry words were traded, but no more shots were fired. The wagon drivers yielded and returned the cargo to the Land Office the following morning.

Three years later, Texas was granted statehood. In 1850, nearly a decade after the Archives War, voters throughout the state endorsed Lamar's choice of Austin as the permanent capital. By the time they took this decisive action, the town's population was nearly six hundred.

Lamar drew up plans for a school system that began with youngsters and ended with a state university. Enormous grants of land were secured to fund the program, and Austin was selected as the site of the future University of Texas.

Dreaming of making Texas a larger nation than it already was, the second president of the new republic organized a military expedition. About three hundred of his soldiers, along with a few civilian traders, were dispatched to Santa Fe. Their mission, Lamar directed, was to persuade residents of that region to transfer their allegiance from Mexico to Texas.

Good maps did not exist in that day, and advisers of the chief executive greatly underestimated the distance to Santa Fe. When the worn-out Texans finally reached the town, instead of being greeted as friends they were met by Mexican soldiers. Within days every member of the Lamar expedition to the New Mexicans was a prisoner, headed to faraway Mexico City on foot.

Some admirers of "good ole Beau" cite his success in ridding the republic of numerous Indians. Critics point to his failure to quell the Comanches and insist that Lamar's only legacy was to plunge Texas in debt.

During the Lamar administration, annual revenues rarely reached $180,000, but the republic's expenditures averaged nearly one million dollars a year. As a result, the president was forced to beg lawmakers to sanction the use of paper currency. By the time he left office, the future of Texas looked grim. When Houston was reelected to the presidency in 1841 he had no ideas of how to make the republic solvent again.

Some accounts say that Lamar came to Texas as a land speculator. Others insist that the former publisher of the *Columbus (Ga.) Enquirer* crossed the Mississippi with the hope of becoming a correspondent for one of the major newspapers of the East. Whatever the case, after his single term as president he devoted his energy to managing his Richmond plantation and soon faded into obscurity.

25
Quanah Parker
The Last Comanche Chieftain

Of all the tribes of the Southwest, none were more problematic for the incoming Texas settlers than the Comanche. They were hunters who followed the buffalo herds and lived a nomadic life on the plains. Stephen F. Austin had arranged treaties with several Comanche tribes and subtribes, but antagonisms were frequent and incidents occurred all along the Texas frontier. One of the most interesting and tragic episodes involved a young blonde-headed, blue-eyed nine-year-old in Central Texas.

In 1834 Elder John Parker brought his clan up the Brazos River and into what was later known as Limestone County. There they found open country and rich soil populated with mostly bear, deer, and wildfowl. The Parkers built a stockade near the Navasota River and soon staked out cornfields. There were no more than two or three other cabins in the area.

On the morning of May 19, 1836, most of the men went to the fields, which were out of sight of the stockade, leaving behind six men and the women and children. About midmorning a large party of Comanche, Kiowa, and Caddoan horsemen arrived at the wall of the stockade, waving a dirty white flag and asking for water and beef.

Benjamin and Silas Parker attempted to negotiate with them, but something went wrong and the warriors attacked them and then turned their fury on the others still inside the stockade. The elder was killed and his wife, Granny Parker, and the other women were assaulted.

The men from the fields came running back with their rifles in hand, and the warriors fled, leaving behind five dead men and several battered women, two of whom later died. The mixed party of warriors, however, took five captives with them: Rachel Plummer and her small son, James; Elizabeth Kellogg; and six-year-old John and nine-year-old Cynthia Ann Parker.

Rachel Plummer was for eighteen months a Comanche slave. She was ransomed later in Santa Fe. During her captivity she bore a child, who was killed. She returned to Texas but died shortly afterward, never seeing her son James again.

Elizabeth Kellogg found better treatment with the Caddoan tribe. She was sold to the Delaware tribe and then ransomed to Sam Houston in December 1836 for $150.

John Parker and Jake Plummer were found and ransomed in 1842. Parker was unable to readjust to life among the settlers. He returned to his tribe to search for his sister. He later married a Mexican girl who had been a Comanche captive, and they lived the rest of their lives in Mexico.

Cynthia Ann Parker, however, was a captive of the Quahadis, the most warlike of the Comanche tribes. Sightings were reported at numerous times, but all efforts to ransom her failed. She became the wife of Peta Nacona, war chief of the Noconi band, and bore him three children: Pecos, Quanah, and Topsanah. In all ways, Cynthia Ann became a Comanche and was given the name Naduah.

Several years later, during the fall of 1860, Peta Nacona led a war party into the area near old Parker's Fort. As he withdrew, Sul Ross, a Texas Ranger, gathered approximately one hundred riders to pursue the war party. These riders were made up of twenty regulars from the Second Cavalry, seventy volunteers, and several Texas Rangers and Tonkawa scouts. When they failed to overtake Peta Nacona immediately, Ross chose to continue the pursuit indefinitely and strike a punitive blow.

On December 17 Ross's Tonkawa scouts discovered Peta Nacona's camp on the Pease River, not far from the site of present-day Quanah. The warriors were hunting, leaving only women, children, and Mexican slaves in camp. Ross's party swept down on the camp, and a massacre ensued. During the fighting, one of the Rangers caught a glimpse of Cynthia Ann's dirty blonde hair and blue eyes. The Rangers "rescued" her and an eighteen-month-old baby.

The Texas settlers fought constant battles against a harsh environment and marauding native tribes who preyed on cattle and sometimes captured and assimilated the children of the settlers, such as Quanah's mother, Cynthia Ann Parker.

When Ross returned with Cynthia Ann, she was identified and even responded to her name, although she spoke no English. Her original family had prospered over the years, becoming one of the state's respected and prominent families. The family took Cynthia Ann back and did everything they could for her. The state legislature also allotted her land and an annual pension of one hundred dollars.

Cynthia Ann, however, had lived among the Comanche for twenty-five years. Her husband and family were Comanche. She could not adjust to living with her original family and tried to escape, which led them to keep her under guard. Her daughter Topsanah died four years after she came to live with the Parkers. Cynthia Ann startled her family by reacting like most Comanche mothers and starving herself to death.

In the meantime, Peta Nacona took no other wife and died from wounds received in a later scrape with Apaches. Pecos died of disease. Quanah, however, matured and demonstrated intelligence and character, so that in his twenties he became the leader of his tribe and eventually the leader of the Comanche in the last great war between the Texas settlers and the region's native tribes. The war was precipitated by the systematic destruction of the great buffalo herds of the plains.

By 1874 the plentiful buffalo herds no longer roamed as widely as they had before. White hunters in search of bison hides had to venture farther south to find their quarry, but the last great buffalo herds were on the Staked Plains, an area protected by treaty from the hunters. Unfortunately, the treaty was not enforced, and the hunters established a base at Adobe Walls, an old trading post that turned into a small fortified town almost overnight.

The native tribes found their primary food source endangered by the random slaughter engineered by the white hunters. As they watched their way of life threatened, prophets rose up in the tribes and called for a general war against the hunters.

Despite having several longstanding feuds with one other, the five tribes of the southern plains—the Quahadi Comanches, the Kiowas, the Kiowa-Apache, the Southern Cheyennes, and the Arapahoes—convened and formed an uneasy alliance. They reached two agreements: they would destroy the buffalo hunters in Texas, and Quanah, chief of the Quahadis, would be their leader. The tribes would form a strike force of seven hundred warriors.

On the night of June 27, 1874, Quanah led the five tribes against Adobe Walls. Twenty-eight hunters and one woman were in the camp that night. Quanah struck at dawn, but he lost the element of surprise when one of the hunters saw the warriors approaching. The tribesmen pressed the attack but fell in large numbers to the men who made their living by shooting accurately and at long range. All of the white hunters wielded .50-caliber Sharps rifles.

Quanah fell wounded but crawled to safety behind a buffalo carcass outside the walls. The warriors laid siege to the camp for three days before retreating. As a result of the loss, the loose tribal alliances fell apart, but separately each tribe carried on the war across five territories and states. Buffalo hunting parties continued to be ambushed until the hunters fled.

The price of this success was the call that all so-called Indians should be placed on reservations, and the U.S. Army was ordered to accomplish that task. There were no more

Artist Georgh Catlin, armed only with the revolver he called Sam, was an avid buffalo hunter. The friction between the native tribes and the white settlers stemmed from the wholesale massacre of the buffalo herds by white hunters. Whereas the buffalo provided so much for the Indian tribes, the whites were mostly interested in the hide, leaving the meat to rot on the plains.

expeditions against the tribes; what followed were calculated, coordinated campaigns to control the tribes. In Texas that task fell to Ranald Mackenzie, a West Point graduate and Civil War veteran. Called Bad Hand by his tribal foes because of a Civil War wound, Mackenzie was admired by his men as the finest Indian-fighting cavalryman in uniform. Before he had come west, he had been assessed by Gen. U. S. Grant as one of the most promising young officers in the army.

Mackenzie was successful in fighting the Comanche because he fought like a Comanche. He had learned that in a war on

Quanah Parker achieved a brief confederation of five tribes to combat the slaughter of the buffalo. The highlight of that union was the attack on Adobe Walls. The price of their success was the relocation of the tribes to reservations and the mandate to the U.S. Army to accomplish that task.

INFORMATION SERVICES DIVISION, TEXAS STATE LIBRARY

the plains, success was defined by finding and destroying your enemy's camp and taking the tribe prisoner. After months of pursuing the Comanches, a captive Comanchero revealed the location of Quanah's camp.

Close to six hundred soldiers struck the camp at Palo Duro on September 28, 1874. Most of the Comanches escaped, but Mackenzie destroyed their supplies and their horses. It was not a flashing-sabers kind of victory, but it was the end of the war because Mackenzie deprived Quanah's warriors of the tools they needed to continue the fight. Without their horses, the tribesmen could neither hunt nor fight. The alliances dissolved. Many walked to the reservations hoping to be fed.

In June 1875 Quanah led the remnants of the Quahadi Comanches to a surrender ceremony at Fort Sill. He was the last Comanche, the last of the southern tribes to surrender. While other tribal chiefs were punished with imprisonment or exile, Quanah held the respect of his former enemy, which most certainly helped his tribe.

Often lauded as the last of the great Comanche chieftains, the son of Cynthia Ann Parker soon organized a delegation to Washington to protest the government's policies that allowed reservation lands to be leased to cattlemen. This 1884 trip was the first of seven that Quanah made to the nation's capital. Usually accompanied by his third wife, Too-nicey, his last Washington visit was in 1905, where he rode in Theodore Roosevelt's inaugural parade along with Geronimo and other distinguished chieftains.

By that time Quanah was considered an elder statesman among his people. A keen businessman, he had built a splendid home about a dozen miles from Fort Sill and speculated in land until he was reputed to be the wealthiest Indian in the United States. In 1910 he considered a presidential inauguration as next to nothing compared with his role in the dedication ceremony when the town of Quanah was formally opened in Hardeman County as a station on the Quanah, Acme, and Pacific Railroad.

By this time highly skilled in the art of political persuasion, the aging chieftain contacted every influential person he knew in Austin and in Washington. It was only right and proper, he urged, that the wife of his father should lie among the Comanches. As a result, the body of Cynthia Ann Parker was exhumed and reinterred at Post Oak Mission, close to her son's home. Quanah died a few months later, on February 21, 1911, at sixty-four years of age.

26
Chester W. Nimitz

Old Graduate

My grandfather's hotel must have had more influence upon me than I realized at the time," Fleet Adm. Chester W. Nimitz of the U.S. Navy once told a group of his subordinates. "Besides, I bear his name—with pride!"

Chester Heinrich Nimitz of Bremen, Germany, formerly captain of a merchant ship, chose Charleston, South Carolina, as his port of entry into the United States in 1843. Parting company with many of his fellow Germans, "Grandpa" later became a captain in the Confederate Army.

In the 1850s he built in Fredericksburg, Texas, "the strangest-looking hotel in the state"—known as the Steamboat Hotel because of its nautical shape. At least four guests of the hotel later became famous. Lt. Col. Robert E. Lee, who served two tours of duty in Texas, enjoyed the hotel several times when duty required him to travel between Fort Mason and other posts. Philip H. Sheridan and James Longstreet were also guests of the Steamboat in the pre–Civil War years. After the war, a civilian from nearby Austin took refuge from the rigors of his job as a bank teller by spending weekends with Grandpa, who never would have guessed that the visitor would later be known as O. Henry.

Nimitz's grandson and namesake, born in 1885, was often brought to Grandpa's hotel for visits, and he soon learned to "walk the corridors as though he were on the deck of a ship." To the disappointment of Grandpa, during his adolescence young Chester began dreaming of an appointment to the U.S. Military Academy. He never made it to West Point, however.

Without his finishing high school, he took a competitive examination for the U.S. Naval Academy at Annapolis, and in 1901 his high score allowed him to go to Annapolis from the Twelfth Congressional District.

Chester graduated seventh in his class of 114 men and was assigned to the USS *Ohio*. Before winning his commission as ensign, the Texan displayed traits that marked him for the rest of his life. Because he questioned some time-honored customs of the U.S. Navy, he was disciplined by being assigned to the submarine *Plunger*. "I'll go without saying a word," he reputedly told a messmate, "but I'll keep on thinking for myself instead of simply doing things the way they've always been done." Very early, Nimitz developed a philosophy of life that included the maxim "Teach me the glorious lesson that occasionally it is possible that I [as well as the top brass] may be mistaken."

Rising gradually through the ranks, by 1913 Nimitz was in command of the Atlantic Submarine Flotilla when U.S. leaders realized that the danger of war was mounting. He was sent to Germany to become familiar with a radical new kind of internal combustion engine that had been invented by Rudolph Diesel.

"This time, you won't be bothered by long-standing traditions," a friend teased when Nimitz was assigned to direct the construction of the U.S. Navy's first diesel-powered submarine. When the work at Groton, Connecticut, was completed, the "Nimitz diesel" was installed in the USS *Maumee* and performed flawlessly.

By 1926 Nimitz had completed special studies at the Naval War College, so he was a natural choice to become the first professor of naval science and tactics when a reserve officer training program was initiated at the University of California at Berkeley. During the three happy years he spent there he did not imagine that his association with the university would continue for the rest of his life.

Just fifteen years after having launched the ROTC program at Berkeley, Nimitz stepped into the vacancy created when Adm. Husband E. Kimmel resigned in the aftermath of the December 7, 1941, Japanese attack on Pearl Harbor. Given command of the Pacific Fleet and the Pacific Ocean Areas, he regretted only that his grandfather had not lived to see him

ADMIRAL NIMITZ STATE HISTORICAL PARK

Sea-loving Chester Heinrich Nimitz (left) had a profound effect upon his namesake and grandson. Grandpa was a little anxious when Chester seemed to set his sights on attending West Point, but he relaxed when his grandson instead was admitted to the U.S. Naval Academy at Annapolis.

become an admiral. At the time of his promotion, Nimitz had never ordered a gun to be fired in hostile action, but eventually he commanded 6,215 ships and 14,847 combat aircraft.

Some have suggested that Nimitz's strategy in the first year of the war shows a distinctive Texas influence. In the previous century, the settlers did not expend all their efforts on mastering vast unbroken tracts of land. Instead, they chose strategic points, created settlements, and then tried to link them by trails.

Charged with guarding Hawaii and the West Coast against another Japanese attack while extending communication to Gen. Douglas MacArthur in Australia, the Texas-reared admiral launched what became known as "island hopping." There was considerable risk in this process, he realized from the start, but Nimitz was not surprised when Japanese naval forces began moving out from New Guinea and the Solomon Islands.

The first major engagement in this theater of war was the battle of the Coral Sea, which stemmed the tide of Japanese advancement for the first time. Quickly the war in the Pacific came to center upon the positioning of the American and Japanese aircraft carriers. Nimitz was one of the first to recognize the value of naval air power and exploit it to his advantage. Thus he was able to block the Japanese threat across the Pacific.

Meanwhile, U.S. intelligence units had succeeded in breaking the Japanese naval code. As a result of this "victory that was won without firing a shot," as Nimitz described it, the Americans knew in advance the composition and approximate destinations of enemy vessels that planned to converge in the central Pacific.

On June 3, 1942, the American and Japanese fleets began a three-day battle near Midway Island. During the engagement the Japanese and American vessels never caught sight of each other. Carrier-based aircraft executed all aspects of the battle. When the battle ended, four Japanese carriers, one cruiser, and one destroyer had been sunk. For the first time in more than three centuries, the Japanese navy had suffered an overwhelming defeat.

Defying conventional military wisdom, Nimitz later sent submarines and light surface units into Japan's inland sea. Shore installations designed to protect Tokyo were bombarded

Close associates remember Adm. Chester W. Nimitz as a commander with a keen sense of humor and a great love of good stories.

NIMITZ LIBRARY, DEPARTMENT OF THE NAVY

and scores of ships were sunk. Meanwhile, immense fleets of bombers took off from island bases gained under the island-hopping direction of Nimitz and made hundreds of strikes against the Japanese main islands. On September 2, 1945, the admiral from Texas escorted Japanese representatives aboard the battleship *Missouri* in Tokyo Bay to sign the documents ending World War II.

Small wonder, therefore, that Nimitz received so many awards after the war. From the United States he received the Distinguished Service Medal with two gold stars. Greece bestowed upon him the Grand Cross of the Order of George I. British leaders pinned upon him the Grand Cross of the Bath. Even Ecuador and China conferred their most distinguished medals upon him. Inevitably, colleges and universities boosted their own prestige by conferring honorary degrees upon the Annapolis graduate. Some of those who count Nimitz as an LL.D. alumnus are Notre Dame, Harvard, Tulane, Northwestern, Williams, California, Hawaii, Syracuse, and

Richmond (Virginia). Returning to the University of California after special service with the United Nations, Nimitz was named regent.

Of all the honors and awards heaped upon him, he frequently downplayed their significance, saying, "Of course I am proud to have been recognized by these distinguished universities. I value all of the parchments that have been handed to me by noted educators. Yet the most treasured piece of such paper that I hold came to me not long after I became a fleet admiral. That's when this dropout from the Kerrville, Texas, high school was given a diploma, making him an honorary graduate."

Part 6

Mavericks, Strays, and Zealots

Gen. Antonio López de Santa Anna had risen to power by revolutionary means, and many pointed out the irony in his lack of sympathy for the revolutionaries in Texas.

27

Gen. Antonio López de Santa Anna

Serene Highness

No one in Texas history is more despised than a Mexican who was a soldier, politician, revolutionary, president, dictator, exile—and cold-blooded killer. Because he gave no quarter to the overwhelmingly outnumbered defenders of the Álamo, Santa Anna's name is today still synonymous with barbarity. That's why some of the fiercest gales that blow in the far West are despised as the Santa Anna winds.

The career of Gen. Antonio López de Santa Anna, whose seesaw movements between obscurity and power have few parallels, began at age fifteen when he became a cadet in the Spanish-led colonial army. After fighting against revolutionists for a decade, he suddenly switched sides.

In 1821, not long after he began aiding the struggle against the Spanish, Mexican independence was won, and Augustín de Iturbide declared himself emperor of the new nation. Santa Anna had expected to be rewarded by appointment as governor of Vera Cruz. When a rival was given the governorship, Santa Anna led a revolt that drove Iturbide from power, then elevated himself to command of all Mexican forces.

In 1829 Spain attempted to reconquer Mexico, but Santa Anna's forces drove the invaders back across the Atlantic Ocean. As a result, in 1832 he was elected president of the republic, which had adopted a federal constitution in 1824.

Now in a position of great power, the native of Jalapa in the province of Vera Cruz assumed dictatorial powers in 1834. His abolition of the constitution infuriated the transplanted Americans in Texas, many of whom would have otherwise been content to be loyal citizens of Mexico.

Some settlers north of the Rio Grande remarked at the "strange inconsistency" of the man who rose to power through revolution but who would not tolerate a similar movement in Texas for independence. Perhaps eager to demonstrate his skill as a strategist, perhaps unwilling to relinquish power to a subordinate, Santa Anna personally led his troops against Texans. Winning the battle at the small mission in San Antonio proved costly. "Remember the Alamo!" became a slogan causing men who knew that defeat meant death to fight like demons. At San Jacinto, against great odds, Sam Houston's men won a dramatic victory and soon made Santa Anna their prisoner.

Among the Texas soldiers at the front and the civilians back home, there was strong feeling that Santa Anna should be executed. Stephen F. Austin, however, who knew what it was like to spend months in a Mexican jail, led a group of colonists who argued that their captive was worth more to them alive than dead.

After prolonged discussion among captors and negotiations with Santa Anna, he agreed to back independence for Texas in return for his life. Although he signed a formal treaty by which Mexico relinquished its most northern state, it was repudiated in Mexico City. Simultaneously, Santa Anna was stripped of power and was forbidden to return to the nation he had helped to form.

Following a short stay in the United States, the former dictator managed to slip back into Mexico, where he lived in quiet obscurity. Word that France was about to seize the former Spanish province gave Santa Anna a fresh opportunity. He took command of all available troops, led them to Vera Cruz, and in 1838 held the port city against powerful French warships.

One of the observers of that action from aboard a foreign warship was David Farragut. He was said to have profited from what he learned there to help him win the battle of Mobile Bay during the American Civil War. On shore, Santa Anna took a direct hit by a French ball and lost a leg. His injury and his victory helped elevate him to power once more. He began calling himself president in October 1841 and soon assumed dictatorial powers again.

An 1843 constitution drafted under his supervision provided for the election of a new president—and guaranteed that he would win the office. Once the post was his, instead of relaxing his hold upon the nation, he strengthened his dic-

Sam Houston resisted strong pressure to execute the Mexican leader after his capture following the battle of San Jacinto.

tatorial powers. Inevitably, his actions led to a new revolution—this time by Mexicans rather than Texans. Driven from office in 1844, the man who had smashed the Alamo fled to Jamaica.

Logically, that should have ended Santa Anna's career. It might have done so, had war with the United States not broken out. In this emergency, his countrymen called their most experienced military leader back home in 1846 and made him their provisional president.

The American forces, however, defeated Santa Anna at Buena Vista, Cerro Gordo, and Chapultepec. When Mexico City fell in 1847, Santa Anna was once more forced out of the country.

The exile lived in Jamaica and Venezuela for five years, then a new emergency in the Mexican government led to his recall and election to a one-year term as president. He used that year to consolidate his power and in December 1853 proclaimed himself president of Mexico for life, with the title of Serene Highness and the right to choose his successor. His serenity was short lived. A revolution broke out early in 1855, and after more than a year of bitter fighting he left Mexico City in the middle of the night. He was permitted to go only after he reluctantly signed his unconditional abdication.

This time he went to Cuba, but after a short stay he returned to Venezuela. Tried by a Mexican court and found guilty of

Political turmoil in Mexico even allowed the French to place one of their own, Ferdinand Maximilian Joseph, on the throne in 1864. His brief rule was abruptly ended by a Mexican firing squad.

treason in absentia, he was safe from the law, but his large estates were confiscated.

Fresh interest in Mexico on the part of France came to a climax during the U.S. Civil War, when Napoleon III invaded the country, planning to make it a base for an American empire. Ferdinand Maximilian Joseph, brother of the emperor of Austria, was put on the throne in 1864 as a puppet emperor. Santa Anna saw this as an opportunity to recoup his leadership, but he was refused admittance to the country.

During his last exile, the one-time foe of Houston lived briefly in the United States, where he became acquainted with William H. Seward. Several letters were exchanged between them before Seward became weary of suggested intrigue and cut off their correspondence.

In the 1860s Santa Anna was exiled from Mexico and, for a time, tried to gain the support of U.S. Secretary of State William H. Seward. Nothing came of those efforts, but in 1874 Santa Anna was allowed to return to Mexico.

LIBRARY OF CONGRESS

Benito Juárez, a Zapotec Indian, led a successful revolt against the French, executed Maximilian, and assumed the presidency. He died in 1872, and in 1874 Santa Anna was allowed to return home as part of a general amnesty.

For the final two years of Santa Anna's life he lived in poverty so dire that he often depended upon charity for his food. Had Sam Houston been alive at the time, he would have said that such an existence was entirely too good for the man whose name was then and still is anathema to every Texan.

28
Andrew Jackson
Political Clout

An aging Andrew Jackson was so badly stooped that he looked three or four inches under his six-foot-one-inch height. Further complicating his health, a bullet was still lodged near his heart from an 1806 duel and occasionally caused him to double over in pain. A rasping cough and frequent abdominal spasms added to his constant discomfort.

For years his unsteady gait had required him to use a stout cane. His last teeth having been lost years earlier, he briefly tried "gumming it," then resorted to an artificial set that never fit properly.

Former presidents have not always continued to focus their time and energy on politics; some who tried have lived to regret that their influence was so little. Such was not the case with Jackson. After leaving the Executive Mansion in 1837, he devoted his remaining thirteen years to many political issues, but he gave priority to Texas and adding the state to the union.

His correspondence is rife with allusions to the task. For example, in a September 18, 1843, letter to his friend and adviser Maj. William B. Lewis, he noted: "That arch enemy, J. Q. Adams, rallied all his forces to prevent it [passage of a bill granting statehood to Texas]. We must regain Texas; *peacebly if we can; forcibly if we must!*"

Time after time, Old Hickory railed against John Quincy Adams, whom he called "deranged or superlatively wicked" and "a reckless old man," despite the fact that he was eight months younger than the Tennessean. Adams, like many in the Northeast, was opposed to making Texas a state because of the slavery issue.

Jackson seldom said much in public about the slavery issue; he preferred to stress the vast amount of land that was available in Texas and to warn that Great Britain wished to acquire the region. Prior to the election of 1844, he warned, "England wants Texas, next Cuba, and then Oregon. [Should this move succeed, Texans would become] hewers of wood and drawers of water [for the English nobility]." Such a turn of events would allow Britain to fashion "an iron hoop about the United States." Hence he urged, "Bring those things which I have expressed to the view of Genl Houston. He has too much patriotism to let Texas become a Colony of England."

Jackson's anxiety was well founded. As president of the Republic of Texas, Sam Houston had offered the republic to the United States on three separate occasions, but annexation was defeated in Congress each time. Angry at this turn of events, some influential voices within the Lone Star Republic counseled negotiations with Britain.

There had been earlier efforts to buy Texas from Mexico. During his administration, John Quincy Adams had offered one million dollars for the region. Martin Van Buren had raised the offer to five million dollars.

Houston entertained the option that Texas could remain independent and extend its boundaries westward to the Pacific. Jackson seized the idea and expanded it, suggesting that "Texas must claim the Californias. The fishing interests of the North and of the East would stop at nothing to obtain a harbor on the Pacific." In return for California he believed that opposition to slavery in Texas would evaporate.

Nevertheless, Jackson's cunning was not enough to win a victory. Anti-Texas voices became more numerous and more strident. Meanwhile, John Tyler, swept into office by the sudden death of William Henry Harrison early in 1841, gave no sign of interest in statehood for Texas.

Old Hickory warned that he would give his last gasp to bring Texas into the Union, and Houston obliged the former president by making his most extraordinary political appointment, naming Jackson a chargé d'affaires to the Republic of Texas.

During the presidential campaign of 1844, Jackson pushed for the nomination of James K. Polk of Tennessee, Speaker of the House of Representatives for seven months but otherwise a political unknown. Jackson, however, pronounced Polk "the

After his presidency Jackson returned to the Hermitage near Nashville and devoted his energies to many causes, especially the annexation of Texas.

right man for the right spot at the right time." On the ninth ballot of the Democratic Convention, Polk received his party's nomination. That November he won the White House.

Anxious for the Texas issue to be resurrected and statehood granted, Jackson continued to exercise all the political clout he held. How influential his efforts might have been, no one knows, for three days before Tyler left office, in a move of doubtful constitutionality, a joint resolution of Congress declared Texas the twenty-eighth state in the Union, pending Texas's consent.

29
Ben McCulloch

A Rare Breed

Half a dozen Texas Rangers sat around a late afternoon campfire drinking coffee, smoking, and talking. One of them stopped in midsentence, pointed a finger at another, and demanded, "Why don't you say something, Ben?"

Ben McCulloch's blue eyes glowed with the reflection of the campfire. He had a strong face that was always kept under perfect control. No one ever knew what was on his mind until he spoke. He was cool—a word that was used to describe many Rangers—and above all he was cool under fire. Like most Rangers, he seemed to think best during the heat of combat. He gave few orders, but those he did were obeyed unquestioningly. McCulloch was one of the best of the select group of men known as Texas Rangers.

No ONE KNOWS precisely why the body of scouts, unofficial lawmen, and soldiers came to be known as the Texas Rangers. Their genesis may have been with the group of ten freelance gunmen hired by Stephen F. Austin in 1823 to protect his settlers from Native American warriors and Mexican bandits. Austin charged them with "ranging" the territory. These ten gunmen had no formal status, but they proved so effective that their number was soon doubled.

By the early nineteenth century the term Ranger had a long history of use in reference to Indian fighters, denoting the kind of gunman who carried the fighting to the enemy. The Rangers' evolution in Texas was strongly influenced by the size of the territory, the government's inability to maintain an army or a

185

large police force, and the two violent frontiers that confronted the settlers. Farmer militias could not defend their homesteads effectively, thus the government provided for their protection by allowing the state's citizens to protect themselves by organizing ranging companies.

The Rangers first took the form of mounted militia. The lack of state funds prevented them from becoming an established, regularized force, but the constant danger on the frontier required the Ranger companies to remain on constant duty. Essentially, the republic authorized the Rangers as a paramilitary force and supported the companies as funds became available. Recruitment and support, however, were local responsibilities.

The lack of state funding and regulation allowed for a kind of raw frontier leadership to flourish. Without the encumbrances of political appointment, the primary qualification for Ranger leadership was the ability to survive. Considering the two primary opponents the Rangers encountered—Indian raiders and Mexican bandits—survival skills dominated the chain of command. Thus the Rangers developed the pattern of following officers of their own choosing, and Ranger captains like W. A. A. "Bigfoot" Wallace, John H. Moore, and Ben McCulloch became legends of the frontier.

TENNESSEE-BORN McCulloch acquired itching feet early in life. His father, who had fought in the Creek War and the War of 1812 as a major, took the family to Alabama when Ben was nine years old. Soon they moved back to Tennessee, this time landing at a homestead not far from the Mississippi River and just thirty miles from Davy Crockett's home.

McCulloch planned to come to Texas as part of Crockett's entourage, but he failed to settle his affairs in time to join his fellow Tennesseans in the Alamo. He did, however, join Sam Houston's army, and on April 21, 1836, he was a gunner of one of the Twin Sisters that opened the battle of San Jacinto. He returned to Tennessee, where he mastered the art of surveying land, and then moved to Texas permanently, where he opened a land office in 1838. For a time he lived in Gonzales.

Never married and having plenty of time on his hands, McCulloch relieved the tedium of daily life by becoming a Ranger in Jack Hays's company in San Antonio. His horse, for

The Texas Rangers were given the task of protecting the settlers venturing into the area at the behest of Stephen E. Austin. They rarely acted in a body like that depicted above except during their service in the Mexican War.

which he said he would not take two hundred dollars in gold, was the envy of his comrades. With a Mexican blanket roll tied behind his saddle, he was ready at an instant's notice to grab ammunition, parched corn, tobacco, and a little salt and hit the trail.

During the summer of 1840, a Penateka raiding party looted the town of Victoria. McCulloch discovered the trail on August 5 and began to follow the party, which numbered approximately five hundred. He gathered volunteers as he went, and when he deduced the Indians' route, he sent messengers calling for every available man to rendezvous at Plum Creek, near the San Marcos River. By the time the Penatekas approached Plum Creek on August 12, a small army of army regulars, militia, volunteers, and locals were in position.

When the Indians saw the mass of men waiting for them, the warriors began to screen the withdrawal of the party that

Col. Jack Hayes was one of the legendary early Texas Rangers. He introduced the Colt revolver into the Ranger armory and was a profound influence on Ben McCulloch.

was laden with the plunder of the raid. The warriors demonstrated their bravery with whoops and by brandishing their weapons until a chieftain, easily identified by his long headdress, rode forward and taunted the Texans by an exhibition of horsemanship.

Several shots struck the chief, and he fell forward in his saddle and was borne away by another rider. At this point the small army of Texans charged. The Penatekas ran from the field, planning on reassembling and ambushing their attackers later. The Indian pack mules, however, had become mired in the creek, and the horses stolen from Victoria overran the fleeing Indians. Those who were not trampled by the herd were shot by Texans patrolling the edge of the bog.

Finally the Penatekas abandoned their loot and fled. The Texans pursued them for ten or twelve miles and then returned to the creek to divide the spoils. Their casualties were one dead and seven wounded, but the Indians lost as many as 130. The loss of their chief and so many warriors dramatically reduced the threat of the Penatekas in the region. Lore of the frontier credited this dramatic victory to the immigrant from Tennessee and his trio of followers—Archie Gibson, Barney Randall, and Alsey Miller.

In 1846 war broke out between Mexico and the United States over Texas, which had been granted statehood in 1845. Gen. Zachary Taylor headed the American army in Texas and asked the state for two regiments of horsemen. The first of these was made up of Rangers, and McCulloch was one of the unit's officers. Joining Taylor's army at Fort Brown on the Rio Grande, McCulloch's Rangers were given the task of scouting the land between Matamoros and Monterey to select the invasion route for the army.

During this first phase of the war, McCulloch's Rangers served in the vanguard of Taylor's army. They smashed through any and all Mexican resistance. The army, however, bogged down outside Monterey, and Taylor negotiated an armistice. During the lull, most of the Rangers returned home, having fulfilled their six-month commitment; some were disgusted with the cessation of hostilities around Monterey.

McCulloch returned in January 1847 when he heard that Taylor had resumed the offensive, but he offered to serve at his own pleasure, not for a specified time. Taylor was desperate for mounted troops and violated regulations by enlisting McCulloch and a company of Rangers on their own terms.

Taylor's first assignment to McCulloch was to find Gen. Antonio López de Santa Anna's army. The Texan took sixteen men, crossed a thirty-mile-span of desert, and found Santa Anna at Encarnación. On February 20, McCulloch returned with seven men to ascertain the size of Santa Anna's army. By counting fires and scouting the camp as he had done at many Comanche camps before, McCulloch determined that at least fifteen thousand Mexican soldiers were bivouacked at Encarnación. He sent word back to Taylor, but he and another Ranger stayed within the Mexican picket line until daybreak. As breakfast fires were being lit, the two Rangers rode through the camp and returned to Taylor.

Meanwhile, Taylor had acted on the information and retreated to a strong defensible position near Buena Vista. Santa Anna, however, interpreted the retreat as a signal to attack and expected to overcome a demoralized American

Ben McCulloch distinguished himself in action during the Mexican War. When Texas seceded, he moved to confiscate arms and ammunition in San Antonio. In light of his Ranger background and war service, he was made a Confederate general in the first month of the Civil War.

army swiftly. Instead, the Mexican army suffered a disastrous defeat, and Santa Anna was forced to lead the remnants of his army back across the desert.

McCulloch and his men returned to Texas. The information they had gathered had enabled Taylor to win an unlikely battle, giving the American general sufficient fame to win a presidential bid two years later.

Returned from the war, McCulloch left Texas for California and the gold rush of 1849. When he failed to find his fortune in gold, he returned to Texas and reverted to his familiar role as lawman and soldier. By the time Confederates fired upon Fort Sumter in Charleston Harbor, he was a colonel in the Texas militia stationed at San Antonio.

When the Lone Star State seceded, McCulloch accepted from Maj. Gen. David E. Twiggs the surrender of the Military Department of Texas. By far the largest surrender of territory in the annals of the U.S. Army, Texans gained more than a score of military bases and vast quantities of weapons, ammunition, and supplies.

Commissioned a brigadier general in the Confederate army in May 1861, McCulloch was placed in command of the Indian

In March 1862 Ben McCulloch, veteran Indian fighter and Texas Ranger, was the most prominent casualty at Elkhorn tavern, or Pea Ridge.

Territory, where he obtained a promise from the Cherokees to fight for the South and arranged for Stand Watie to organize a Cherokee force. Sent to Missouri, on August 10, 1861, he won a major victory at Wilson's Creek. Always a maverick, McCulloch scorned uniforms and usually wore a black velvet suit in the field.

During the following spring, the second-ranking brigadier general in Confederate forces led his brigade against men in blue at Elkhorn Tavern (or Pea Ridge), Arkansas. There McCulloch reverted to his favorite role as scout and personally set out to reconnoiter the Federal lines. Pvt. Peter Pelican, a Yankee sharpshooter, caught McCulloch in his sight, and the single shot of an inexperienced Union soldier killed a man who had previously dodged hundreds of Indian arrows and thousands of Mexican bullets.

30
John R. Brinkley
500,000 Watts

Every time I've said anything about moving south, you start putting up objections."

"That's because I really like small-town life," responded an aide to Dr. John R. Brinkley. "I don't have a thing against Oklahoma City, but I like Milford."

"Who said anything about Oklahoma City?" exploded his employer. "I've about made up my mind to relocate somewhere in Texas, close to the Mexican border."

"It's like a desert there. Growing up in the Smoky Mountains, you might find yourself homesick for the sight of a hill—"

"Bunk!" interrupted the internationally known surgeon. "I've been thinking about Texas for a long time; lots of my patients have come from there."

"Kansas is maybe the only state in the union where you can keep your clinic going," ventured his subordinate.

"People who say that don't know what they're talking about. Many Texas towns are half an hour or less from Mexico, and there's no medical association there," explained the surgeon.

That conversation was soon followed by action. With the Kansas Medical Association making things hot for the physician, he closed the doors of his clinic and put his elegant mansion up for sale before moving to Del Rio, Texas.

Fond of saying that he looked to the future instead of the past, Brinkley's new interest was in radio, "the coming thing." Although he had already found an audience through radio station KFKB, once in Texas, Brinkley intended to sink part of his sizable fortune in a radio station powerful enough to reach a

*North Carolina native
Dr. John Romulus Brinkley.*

much larger constituency. Because Texas had regulations that might prove troublesome, he intended to build his station just across the border in Mexico, where labor was also cheap.

Once station XER went on the air, Brinkley began making pitches of the sort that later would be associated with radio evangelists. "Waiving any and all fees, I will be glad to answer any medical question that you wish to send me," he told his listeners in his best bedside manner. "But you must remember that I cannot handle my enormous volume of correspondence without the help of secretaries. They have to be paid, of course. Even at two cents per letter, you would be surprised at the size of my monthly bill for postage stamps. So I have to ask you, my faithful listeners, to enclose two one-dollar bills in each letter that you wish me to answer."

There are no records to indicate how many of Brinkley's listeners sent the token fees along with their medical questions, but the number must have been substantial since the power of Brinkley's new communication system was boosted several times and eventually reached half a million watts. As the most

Brinkley's Milford, Kansas, residence.

powerful radio station in the world, it could be heard clearly throughout most of North America and soon generated a new demand for the services of the physician who called himself "a pioneer, far in advance of conventional medicine."

Naturally, he said little to his radio audience or anyone else about his early years or his medical training. Born in mountain-ous Jackson County, North Carolina, as a young man he served a stint as a rural mail carrier. Brinkley noticed that some of his patrons regularly received letters from correspondence schools, and that may have triggered his interest in the Eclectic Medical University of Kansas City. From that institution, he received what it called a medical degree.

It was a simple procedure for Brinkley to apply for a license to practice medicine in Arkansas. Once he had the Arkansas license, he gained licenses for Tennessee, Connecticut, and Kansas.

Late in 1917 the young "physician," dressed in stark white with a stethoscope around his neck, opened his practice in

While a member of the family undergoes Brinkley's questionable treatment for impotence, relatives wait at the gate of the Brinkley Hospital.

Milford, Kansas. He chose Milford because it had no resident physician at the time and was a considerable distance from the nearest hospital.

Early in his medical practice, the mail-order M.D. encountered a few men who were impotent or who suffered from waning sexual prowess. Brinkley believed that goats were the most sexually potent of animals, and he reasoned there should be some way to put this information to good use.

Long before the first bone marrow or organ transplant, Brinkley made a startling announcement. Extensive experimentation had shown, he said, that the testicles of young goats could be transplanted into impotent humans. This surgery, he said, made formerly impotent men behave like twenty-year-olds.

Naturally, he maintained a strict secrecy about his surgical procedures. If his immensely valuable discoveries were made public, he told the press, "Half the doctors west of the Mississippi River would open clinics and compete with me."

Business began to boom at his dispensary. Men scrambled over one another in their haste to pay two hundred dollars for

A mob of about twenty thousand gathered to protest the closing of Brinkley's powerful radio station.

goat glands. So many patients clamored for help from Brinkley that he borrowed money and built a fifty-bed hospital. Uncertain about the course of his future, he secured licenses in Texas and other states.

By 1921 Brinkley was considered by ordinary folk as one of the wonders of the medical world. The cost of his procedure escalated to fifteen hundred dollars, yet each Monday morning prospective patients formed a line that stretched to the gates of the hospital.

Inevitably, Brinkley came to the attention of the American Medical Association. Exposed as a quack who preyed upon gullible men, he struck back by launching a suit for damages against a doctor who had been critical of Brinkley's procedures.

This and other litigations signaled the end for Brinkley's practice. By the time his Kansas license was revoked, he was ready to launch his radio station in Mexico and had plans to develop a new hospital there. A stream of complaints from the American Medical Association channeled through the U.S.

State Department convinced Mexican authorities that they should shut down the station. By that time, Brinkley faced so many lawsuits that he reluctantly took his Arkansas medical diploma from the wall and abandoned surgery.

Filing for bankruptcy, he seemed to have hidden from the courts much of his estimated fortune of twelve million dollars. Earlier, he had campaigned to become governor of Kansas and had nearly succeeded. Now he ran for a Texas seat in the U.S. Congress. He was defeated, ending the meteoric career of "the greatest charlatan in the annals of American medicine."

Brinkley's death did not put an end to his influence, however. In 1934, congressmen fashioned and passed a Communications Act of 1934 that is a monument of sorts to the North Carolina native whose radio station touted the benefits of "goat gland surgery" throughout North America.

31
Jefferson Davis
Ships of the Desert

U.S. Secretary of War Jefferson Davis, a stickler for details, wrote a voluminous document as his first annual report to President Franklin Pierce. Dated December 1, 1853, it detailed scores of activities in which he had been engaged since taking office.

Among the more important ones were several District of Columbia projects: The extension of the Capitol had been roofed in, but there was no estimate of how long it would take to erect a dome over the building; the ceilings of the Senate and House chambers had been finished, but work on an aqueduct to supply water for Washington City had been suspended for lack of funds.

Having dealt with these matters he knew to be of interest to the president, Davis turned to one of his own pet projects. He had been right, he assured the chief executive, in his belief that camels would prove invaluable as beasts of burden in the great Southwest. To buttress his conclusion he wrote: "Napoleon when in Egypt used with marked success the dromedary in subduing the Arabs whose habits and country were very similar to those of the mounted Indians of our Western plains. France is about to adopt the dromedary in Algeria. For like military purposes, for expresses [rapid transportation of messages and goods] and for reconnaissances, it is believed, the dromedary will supply a want now seriously felt in our [military] service."

Davis did not inform the president that "the great camel experiment," centered in Texas, was a subject of ridicule by his

198

Jefferson Davis, later president of the Confederacy, is widely considered to have been one of the most competent secretaries of war to serve the nation.

political rivals. Friends and foes alike, however, agreed that the secretary of war "never turned an idea loose, once he had a rope around its neck."

One of his earliest recorded speeches in which Davis advocated the use of camels in the West was delivered in the U.S. Senate in 1851. He had never seen a camel of any variety, but he had studied the literature on these animals with great care. Hence he was certain that dromedaries could be of great service in what he called "our great deserts, which remain largely unexplored."

Once he entered the cabinet of Franklin Pierce, he dispatched a delegation of army offices to the Crimea to observe the war going on there and to make a detailed report on the habits, uses, and availability of camels. Soon after their report was submitted, Davis wheedled from Congress a special appropriation of thirty thousand dollars for the purchase of camels.

It took several months to negotiate the purchase of a herd of camels at the average cost of $250 per animal. After

A balky camel gave its handlers every indication of being unwilling to go to Texas.

a tempestuous ninety-day voyage from the Mediterranean to the Gulf Coast, the animals and men landed at Indianola, Texas, on May 14, 1856.

Aided by camel drivers whom he had hired while abroad, Maj. Henry C. Wayne drove the animals overland for more than a week. He then established a base for the U.S. Camel Corps at Camp Verde, about sixty miles northwest of San Antonio.

By the time the animals were stabled in Camp Verde, the original transport vessel was again en route to Egypt to buy more camels. With the benefit of the experience of the first purchase accomplished, this second procurement mission secured forty-four animals rather quickly. When the second shipment of camels was ready to disembark at Indianola, Wayne's camel soldiers were beginning to study a manual on the care and use of camels. It had come to them as the result of the midnight labors of Davis, who translated the French-language original for use in his Camel Corps.

Although camels are notoriously mean and stubborn, they were judged by Davis to be just right for special uses. The U.S. Army was responsible for much of the work involved in exploring the Southwest, a region where the heat was often too much for horses or mules. It was vital, Davis believed, to find a practical southern route for a railroad to the Pacific Ocean. Some northern investors were already laying out a northern

Despite the end of the camel experiment in 1856, an army exploration party was still using camels during the late 1870s.

route, and it would be first to be funded unless Texas and the areas to its west could be charted.

It is not known how many forays into deserts and other then-unknown places were made by the camels and their drivers who fanned out from their base at Camp Verde. This much is certain, however: Knowledge of the West expanded considerably while the sturdy animals were in constant use.

John B. Floyd of Virginia, who succeeded Davis as secretary of war in 1857, allowed the great camel experiment to wither away. The animals that had been brought from the Near East were dispersed to several army camps and no more were purchased. After civil war broke out, official Washington wanted nothing to do with a project launched by Davis, now president of the Confederacy.

32
Ross Perot

Never Give Up!

During the 1996 presidential campaign many a Republican and hosts of Democrats wanted billionaire third-party candidate Ross Perot to withdraw from the race. Few, however, expected him to do so. To quit would have been completely out of character for the man of many slogans, one of which was "Never, never, *never* give up!"

Though much of his adult life has been spent in Texas, the little man with the squeaky voice who became the Pied Piper of modern politics barely made the roster as a native son of the Lone Star State. He first saw the light of day on the Texas side of Texarkana, a city whose name reveals that it straddles the border between Texas and Arkansas.

His father, for whom he was named, bought and sold cotton and provided comfortably for his family. That did not prevent seven-year-old Ross from starting to hustle for dimes, quarters, and dollars on his own. He was an entrepreneur by the time he was in the second grade.

Entering the job market as his own boss, he bought and sold Christmas cards, packets of seeds, gear for horses, and later, calves and then horses. When he was not selling in his hometown during the years before World War II, he was busy delivering newspapers and making weekly collections from his customers.

At the U.S. Naval Academy, the small-in-stature Perot became a "big man on the campus," winning election as president of his class of nearly one thousand young men. He also won appointment as chairman of the Honor Committee, and he served a term as battalion commander.

After graduation Perot fulfilled his four-year service requirement with the navy and married Margot Birmingham of Greensburg, Pennsylvania. When he was discharged, he reverted to his boyhood pursuits and became a salesman again. This time, however, his sales pitch did not focus on cucumber seeds or Norman Rockwell scenes. Living in Dallas, he sold the services of the processing division of the International Business Machines Company (IBM).

Perot became a top salesman, and he also mastered the skills required to run the division in which he worked. Meanwhile, Margot worked as a teacher and put aside a few dollars from every paycheck to accumulate a little nest egg. From it she lent her husband one thousand dollars in 1962 and encouraged him to "Go to it!" He launched Electronic Data Systems Leasing Company (EDS), a brash little competitor of the IBM division in which he had learned the tricks of the trade.

At the head of his own company at age thirty-two, the salesman from Dallas landed the account of a radio company in Cedar Rapids, Iowa. It was a start. Big accounts came a bit later. By the time he had carved out a niche for himself, Perot was busy directing the creation of computer software. "There's a big and a growing market here," he reasoned. "Somebody's gonna develop the tools to handle big batches of information; I may as well beat my competition to the prize."

After having grabbed many prizes, Perot was a man to reckon with, not simply in the field of data processing, but anywhere he entered competition. Just sixteen years after having made his start with a schoolteacher's savings, Perot's name was familiar throughout much of the world.

It became more familiar as the result of an international incident. The passports of two EDS employees were seized late in 1978 by Iranian police and their holders thrown in jail. There was sufficient evidence to conclude that the Iranians wanted to ransom the men for twelve million dollars.

Perot and EDS could have paid the ransom, but instead he bank rolled a rescue team of EDS specialists and sent them to Iran, where they successfully extracted the two hostages. The dramatic rescue inspired author Ken Follett, whose best-selling novel *On Wings of Eagles* was translated into a television

Midshipman Ross Perot of the U.S. Navy, not yet seeing himself as a future data tycoon, thought of the White House as a place he would like to visit some day.

U S NAVAL ACADEMY: DEPARTMENT OF THE NAVY

miniseries. As a result, Perot's prestige rose among garden-variety Americans.

EDS became so large and so profitable that it was a natural target for a takeover. Several corporations were interested, but General Motors prevailed in the bidding for EDS. Not long after Perot ceased to be a CEO and began to function as a GM executive, he quarreled with GM's top management and severed his ties with the corporation.

Having more money than he had imagined he could ever accumulate, Perot was briefly without a company to head. In 1988 he organized Perot Systems Corporation as a competitor of the EDS subsidiary of General Motors.

Long a rasping critic of the federal government and its bureaucracies, in 1992 Perot sensed that George Bush had lost all credibility with the American public. Perot had more money than he could spend and an abiding distrust of the federal bureaucracy. He firmly believed that the government no longer heard what the American public wanted or needed. The Texas billionaire caught another breathtaking glimpse of yet another peak to scale. A fellow raised in Texarkana would run for the White House and redirect the nation away from the path to destruction.

By the time candidate Perot took to a self-financed television campaign in 1992, he had collected—and habitually used—so many slogans and brief challenges that some of them seemed to erupt effortlessly whenever he opened his mouth:

Anybody who's got a lot of money to throw around is inclined to let it solve his problems.

Every good and excellent thing stands moment by moment on the razor's edge of uncertainty and can be gained only by fighting for it.

Only when you surround yourself with men and women of greater capability than your own will exciting things start to happen.

If we don't stop our binge of big spending, this nation will go down the drain.

Always feed the troops first and let their officers come second.

If I could wish one thing for my children it's to leave the American Dream intact.

Nobody has ever crossed a river by going halfway over it.

Now is the time to make the Congress, the White House, the Pentagon, and all of the federal agencies sensitive to you ordinary people—you hard-working folks who own this country.

Vowing that he was ready and willing to spend $350 million of his own money to win the White House and straighten out the nation, campaign records show that he did not go nearly that far in 1992. After parting with more money that most persons earn in a lifetime, the returns on election night would have whittled the presidential candidate down to size—had he been capable of being chastened.

Down but far from out, Perot tried for the presidency again in 1996—this time dipping deep into the pool of money created by "ordinary folk who own this country" and who contribute to the federal campaign fund when they file their income tax returns. Measured by the estimated size of his fortune, the amount he poured into his second try for the White House was a pittance.

Had he won, the Texan would surely have kept his word concerning major issues. He would have made an all-out effort to "make elected officials responsive to the people who own this country," to reduce the national debt, and to downscale a vast number of federal agencies and programs.

Since he was seldom specific about precisely where he would make budget cuts and how deep they would go, there's no guarantee that Perot would have slashed budgets evenly, straight across the board. After all, his first millions were gained as profit from EDS processing of the massive paperwork generated by the U.S. Postal Service, Medicare, and Medicaid.

Bibliography

Allen, Bob. *Waylon & Willie.* New York: Quick Fox, 1979.

American History Illustrated, May 1986.

American Insurance Association Archives.

American Red Cross Archives.

American State Papers: Public Lands, vol. 7.

Austin American-Statesman, 1985–97.

Barker, Eugene C. *Stephen F. Austin.* Austin: University of Texas Press, 1926.

Barr, Alwyn. *Black Texans.* Austin: Jenkins, 1973.

Basler, Roy P., ed. *The Collected Works of Abraham Lincoln.* 9 vols. New Brunswick, N.J.: Rutgers University Press, 1953–55.

Bauer, K. Jack. *The Mexican War.* Lincoln: University of Nebraska Press, 1974.

Baugh, Virgil E. *Rendezvous at the Alamo.* Lincoln: University of Nebraska Press, 1960.

Blansfield, Karen C. *Cheap Rooms and Restless Hearts.* Bowling Green, Ohio: Popular Press, 1988.

Bryant, Ira B. *Barbara Charline Jordan.* Houston: D. Armstrong, 1977.

Buell, Clarence C., and Robert U. Johnson, eds. *Battles and Leaders of the Civil War.* 4 vols. New York: Century, 1884–88. Reprint, Secaucus, N.J.: Castle, 1985.

Carroll, John M., ed. *The Black Military Experience in the West.* New York: Liveright, 1971.

Civil War Times Illustrated, December 1973.

Clements, John. *Texas Facts.* Dallas: Clements Research, 1988.

Confederate Veteran, vols. 4, 5, 18, and 21.

Connor, Seymour V. *Texas.* New York: Crowell, 1971.

Current, Richard N., ed. *Encyclopedia of the Confederacy.* 4 vols. New York: Simon & Schuster, 1993.

Current Biography, 1955–97.

Current-Garcia, Eugene. *O. Henry.* New York: Twayne, 1965.

Dallas Morning News, 1985–97.

Davis, William C. *Jefferson Davis.* New York: HarperCollins, 1991.

De Grummond, Lena Y., and Lynn de Grummond Delaune. *Babe Didrickson*. Indianapolis: Bobbs-Merrill, 1963.

Denisoff, R. Sege. *Waylon*. New York: St. Martin's, 1984.

Dethloff, Henry C. *A Pictorial History of Texas*. College Station: Texas A&M University Press, 1975.

Driskill, Frank A., and Dede W. Casad. *Chester W. Nimitz: Admiral of the Hills*. N.p.p.: Sunbelt Media, 1983.

Edwards, William B. *Story of Colt's Revolvers*. Harrisburg, Pa.: Stackpole, 1953.

Evans, ed. *Confederate Military History*, vol. 15.

Felmly, Bradford K. *Suffering to Silence: 29th Texas Cavalry, CSA*. Quanah, Tex.: Nortex, 1975.

Freeman, Douglas Southall. *R. E. Lee*. 4 vols. New York: Scribner's, 1935–49.

Gallico, Paul. *The Golden Apple*. New York: Doubleday, 1965.

Georgia Historical Quarterly, vols. 2, 10, 13, 20, 24, 27, 33, 34, 51, 57.

Gersch, Harry. *Women Who Made America Great*. New York: Lippincott, 1962.

Halley, James L. *Texas*. Garden City: Doubleday, 1985.

Hamilton, Holman. *Zachary Taylor*. Indianapolis: Bobbs-Merrill, 1951.

Hanighen, Franks C. *Santa Anna*. New York: Coward-McCann, 1996.

Hardin, Stephen L. *Texian Iliad*. Austin: University of Texas Press, 1994.

Haskins, James. *Barbara Jordan*. New York: Dial, 1977.

Henry, Robert S. *The Story of the Mexican War*. New York: Ungar, 1961.

Hill, Edward E. *The Office of Indian Affairs, 1824–1880*. New York: Clearwater, 1974.

Hoehling, A. A. *Disaster*. N.Y.: Hawthorn, 1973.

Houston Post, 1972–76.

James, Marquis. *The Life of Andrew Jackson*. 3 vols. Indianapolis: Bobbs-Merrill, 1933–38.

———. *The Raven*. Indianapolis: Bobbs-Merrill, 1929.

Jennings, Waylon, with Lenny Kaye. *Waylon: An Autobiography*. New York: Warner, 1996.

Journal of Popular Culture, Summer 1991.

Journal of the Southern Historical Society, vol. 24.

Kartman, Ben, and Leonard Brown, eds. *Disaster*. Freeport, N.Y.: Books for Libraries, 1948.

Land: A History of the Texas General Land Office. Austin: The Texas General Land Office, 1992.

Frank Leslie's Weekly Newspaper. September 29, 1900.

Lewis, Willie N. *Between Sun and Sod*. College Station: Texas A&M University Press, 1976.

Lyndon Baines Johnson Library, Oral History Department, interviews.

McElroy, Robert. *Jefferson Davis.* New York: Smithmark: 1995.

McKinley, Silas B. *Old Rough and Ready.* New York: Vanguard, 1946.

Marsh, Carole. *The Big Bio of Ross Perot.* Atlanta: Gallopade, 1995.

Mason, Herbert M., Jr. *Death from the Sea.* New York: Dial, 1972.

Mason, Todd. *Perot—An Unauthorized Biography.* Homewood, Ill.: Business One, 1995.

May, Julian. *Quanah, Leader of the Comanche.* Mankato, Minn.: Creative Educational Society, 1973.

Meyer, Michael. *The Alexander Complex.* Homewood, Ill.: Business One, 1990.

Monsanto Chemical Company archives.

Montgomery, Ruth. *Mrs. LBJ.* New York: Holt, Rinehart and Winston, 1991.

Myers, John B. *The Alamo.* New York: Dutton, 1948.

National Cyclopedia of American Biography. 69 vols. Reprint, Ann Arbor: University Microfilms, 1967.

Naval Historical Center, Archives.

Nevins, Allan. *Ordeal of the Union.* 2 vols. New York: Scribner's, 1947.

New York Tribune, January 14, 1874 (obituary).

Nicolay, John G., and John Hay. *Abraham Lincoln: A History.* 10 vols. New York: Century, 1890.

Paradis, Adrian. *Gail Borden.* Indianapolis: Bobbs-Merrill, 1964.

Porter, William S. *Best Short Stories.* New York: Modern Library, 1945.

———. *Complete Works.* 2 vols. Garden City: Doubleday, 1953.

———. *Whirligigs.* New York: Doubleday, 1910.

Potter, E. B. *Nimitz.* Annapolis: Naval Institute Press, 1977.

Rather, Dan, with Mickey Herskowitz. *The Camera Never Blinks.* New York: Morrow, 1977.

———, with Mickey Herskowitz. *The Camera Never Blinks Twice.* New York: Morrow, 1994.

———, with Peter Wyden. *I Remember.* Boston: Little, Brown, 1991.

Ratliffe, Harold V. *Paths to Glory: Great Men and Women in Texas Sports History.* Waco: Word, 1972.

Reese, James V. *Texas.* Austin: Benson, 1972.

Resler, Ansel H.. "The Impact of John R. Brinkley on Broadcasting in the United States." Ph.D. dissertation. Ann Arbor: University Microfilms, 1959.

Richards, Ann. *Straight from the Heart.* New York: Simon & Schuster, 1989.

Seale, William. *Texas in Our Time.* Dallas: Hendrick-Long, 1972,

Siegel, Stanley, comp. *Selected Readings in Texas History.* Berkeley, Calif.: McCutchan, 1970.

Simpson, Harold B. *Hood's Texas Brigade.* Waco: Texian, 1970.

South Carolina Historical and Genealogical Magazine, 1909.

Southern Historical Society Papers, vols. 9, 35.

Southwestern Historical Quarterly, vol. 23.

Stuart, David. *O. Henry.* Chelsea, Mich.: Scarborough House, 1990.

Sigel, Dorothy S. *Ann Richards.* Springfield, N.J.: Enslow, 1996.

Texas Historical Association Quarterly, vols. 1, 4, 8.

Texas State Travel Guide. Austin: Texas Department of Transportation, 1996.

Toepperwein, Fritz A. *O. Henry Almanac.* Boerne, Tex.: Highland, 1966.

U.S. Army Corps of Engineers, Galveston District.

U.S. Navy Department. *Official Records of the Union and Confederate Navies in the War of the Rebellion.* 31 vols. Washington, D.C.: Government Printing Office, 1894–1927.

U.S. Statutes at Large, vol. 5.

U.S. War Department. *The War of the Rebellion: A Compilation of the Official Records of the Union and Confederate Armies.* 128 vols. Washington, D.C.: Government Printing Office, 1880–1901.

University of Texas, Austin, Ayer Collection, Newberry Library.

Warner, Ezra J. *Generals in Blue.* Baton Rouge: University of Louisiana Press, 1959.

Washington Post, 1966–74.

Webb, Walter P. *The Texas Rangers.* Austin: University of Texas Press, 1935.

Western Carolina University, Special Collections Department of Hunter Library.

Weems, John E. *A Weekend in September.* College Station: Texas A&M University Press, 1980.

Zaharias, Babe Didrikson, with Harry Paxton. *This Life I've Led.* New York: Barnes, 1955.

Index

Illustrations are noted by **boldface.**

Adams, John Quincy, 182–83
admission to U.S., 66–70
Adobe Walls, Tex., 165
Alamo, the, 16, 42, 83, 84, 94, 96, 103–9, **107, 108,** 130, 132, 133, 178
Albright, Richie, 35
Alexandria, Va., 146
Allen, Eliza, 80–81
Allsup, Tommy, 35
Alpert, Herb, 37
Amateur Athletic Union, 26
American Medical Association, 196
American Red Cross, 49
Anahuac, 16
Apaches, 164
Appomattox Court House, Va., 98
Arapahoes, 165
Archives War, 159–60
Arizona, 70, 134
Arizona, USS, 153–54
Arlington, Va., 143, 145
Army of Northern Virginia, 98
Associated Press, 28
Astaire, Fred, 41
Atkins, Chet, 36
Atlanta, Ga., 40
Atlantic Submarine Flotilla, 170
Austin, Moses, 12, 13
Austin, Stephen F., 10, 11–17, 30, 129, 162, 178, 185

Austin, Tex., 17, 42, 73–76, 89, 141, 156, 159, 160 (*see also* San Felipe de Austin)
Austin County, 17
Australia, 172
Autry, Gene, 38

Bailey, George H., 150–51
Banks, Nathanael P., 154
Barret, Theodore H., 98–99
Barton, Clara, 63
Bass, D. M., 138
Baton Rouge, La., 39
Baumgartner, Harry, 47
Baylor, John R., 136
Baylor University, 42
Bayou City, 118–19
Beaumont, Tex., 25
Bellville, Tex., 17
Benjamin Franklin, 87
Bexar District, 34
Birmingham, Margot, 203
Blair, Francis P., 146
blockade-runners, 121
Boca Chica, 98
Boehringer, Emma, 53
Booth, John Wilkes, 98
Borden County, 34
Borden, Gail, 29–34, **34**
Borden, Thomas, 30
Borden, Penelope, 29
Boritt, Gabor, 39
Boston, Mass., 20, 113

Boston University, 113
Bowie, Jim, 83, 104–8, **105**
Bowie knife, 105
Bowles, Colonel, 157
Boyers, Thomas, 81
Branson, David, 99–100
Brazoria, 16
Brazos Santiago, 97–98, 100, 102, 146
Brazos Santiago Island (*see* Brazos Santiago)
Brazos River, 87, 130, 162
Bremen, Germany, 169
Brinkley, John R., 192–97, **193**
Brinkley Hospital, 195, **196**
Brinkley residence, **194**
British Women's Amateur Golf Tournament, 28
Brooklyn, USS, 119
Brown, John, 143, **147**
Brown, S. T., 93
Brownsville, Tex., 97–98
Buena Vista, Mex., **69**, 179, 189
buffalo, 165, **166**
Buffalo Bayou, Tex., 83, 133
Burnet, David G., 129
Burns, Ken, 39
Bush, George, 42, 204
Bush, George W., 44
Butler, Benjamin F., 21, 116
Butler, John C., 86

Caddoan, 162
Caddos, 157
Calcutta, 20
California, 66, 70, 134, 190
camels, 198–201, 200, **201**
Camp Colorado, 146
Camp Cooper, 146
Camp Verde, 200–201
Campeachy, 58
Canby, Edward R. S., 135–38, **138**
Carson, Christopher "Kit," 137
Casa Mata, 69

Cash, Johnny, 38
Cass, Lewis, 70
Castrillon, Manuel, 133
Catherwood, Ethel, 27
Catholicism, Roman, 16, 82
Catlin, George, **166**
CBS *Evening News*, 128
CBS *Reports*, 128
Cedar Rapids, Mich., 203
Cerro Gordo, Mexico, 69, 179
Chapultepec, Mexico, 69, 179
Charleston, South Carolina, 102, 169, 190
Cherokees, 11, 36, 79–81, 157, 192
Cheyennes, Southern, 165
Chicago, Ill., 13, 26
China, 173
Churubusco, Mexico, 69
citizenship, Mexican, 82, 177
city manager, 65
Civil War, 24, 33, 84, 97–102, 115–21, 135–38, 141–48, 149–55, 185–91
Clay, Henry, 70
Clear Lake, 35
Clifton, USS, 117, 119, 151–54
Cline, Isaac, 60
Clinton, Bill, 47
Cohuila province, 15, 103
Colorado, 70, 134
Colorado River, 90, 159
Colquitt, Oscar B., 89
Colt mansion, 24
Colt, Samuel P., 18–24, **20**
Colter, Jessie, 35
Columbia, Tex., 159
Columbus, Ga., 85, 87
Columbus (Ga.) Enquirer, 161
Columbus, Ohio, 76
Comanches, 19, 36, 158–59, 162–67
Comanches, Quahadi, 165–66
Committee of Public Safety, 141
Communications Act of 1934,

197
Concepcion, 88, 103
Confederate Military District of Texas, 97
Confederate Military District of Texas, New Mexico, and Arizona, 116
Contreras, Mexico, 69
Copano, Tex., 93
Coral Sea, 172
Cos, Martin Perfecto, 130–31
cotton, 18, 98, 153
Coubertin, Baron Pierre de, 26
Cranson, Maurine, 53
Crawford County, Ga., 85, 87
Creeks, 157, 186
Crimea, 199
Crocker, Frederick, 150
Crockett, Davy, 105–8, 186
Crystal Palace Exposition of 1851, 29
Crystal Palace Exposition of 1893, **23**
Cuba, 179
Cumberland River, 80
Cunningham, Hugh, 123
Custis, George Washington Parke, 145

Dallas, Tex., 26, 50, 124, 203
Dane, Henry C., 149
Davis, Jefferson, 120, 138, 143, 150, 155, 198–201, **199**
Davis Guard, 150, 155
Davis Guard Medal, **154**
Debray, X. B., 115
Declaration of Independence, Texas, 89
De Guillebon, Charles, 46, 48
Del Rio, Tex., 192
Delawares, 157, 163
Delco, Wilhemina, 43
Denver, Colo., 47
Department of the Gulf, 154

Dickinson, Almeron, 106
Dickinson, Susanna, 108
Didrikson, Mildred "Babe," 25–28, **27**
Diesel, Rudolph, 170
Distinguished Service Medal, 173
District of Columbia, 198
Dodson, Sarah, 86–87
Dowling, Richard, 150–5, 154–55
Dreaming My Dreams, 38
Drennan, Emily, 81

Ecuador, 173
Edison, Thomas, 33
Egypt, 198
Ehrlichman, John, 125
Electronic Data Systems Leasing Company, 203
Eleventh Texas Infantry, 101
Elkhorn Tavern, Ark., **191**
Elmwood Plantation, 89
Emory, William, 150
empresario, 13–17
England, 157, 183
evaporator, vacuum pan, **32.**
Fannin, James W., 87–88, 90–94, **91**, 129
Fargo, N.D., 35
Farragut, David G., 97, 119, 149, 178
Federal Communications Commission, 56
First Cavalry, U.S. Army, 143
First Infantry, U.S. Army, 146
flag, Lone Star, 85–89
flag, Texas, 8, 88, 106
Flint River, 89
Floyd, John B., 201
Folk Country, 37
Follett, Ken, 203
Foote, Shelby, 39
Ford, Gerald, 111
Ford, John S. "Rip," 98–101, 142

Fort Brown, Tex., 189
Fort Craig, N.M., 136
Fort Grigsby, Tex., 149–50
Fort Mason, Tex., 142–44, 169
Fort Sill, Okla., 159, 167–68
Fort Sumter, S.C., 190
Fort Worth, Tex., 28
48 Hours, 128
Fourth Regiment,Texas Mounted
    Volunteers, 135
Fourth Texas Cavalry, 136
Fourth Texas Mounted
    Volunteers, 138
France, 149, 157, 178
Franklin, William B., 150
Fredericksburg, Tex., 169
French, 181

Gallatin, Tenn., 81, 135
Galveston, Tex., 31, 58–65, 63, 64,
    115–21, 116, 118, 120, 124, 141
Galveston Bay, 47, 157
Galveston Bay and Texas Land
    Co., 82, 83
Galveston Channel, 65
Galveston City Company, 31
Galveston District, 65
Galveston News, 63
Galvez, Fernando de, 58, 60
Galvez Island, Tex., 58–59
General Motors Corporation, 204
Georgia, 85–88, 94
Georgia Battalion, 88–89, 92
Gibson, Archie, 189
Glenn, John, 111
Goliad, Tex., 83, 84, 90–94, 92, 94,
    130, 132, 133
Goliad massacre, 93–94
Gonzales, 16, 87, 103, 107, 186
Good Friday, 98
Good Hope Baptist Church, 112
Grammy award, 37
Grand Cross of the Bath, 173
Grand Cross of the Order of

George I, 173
Grandcamp, 46–48
Granite City, 154
Grant, U. S., 67, 98, 166
Greece, 173
Greensboro, N.C., 71, 73
Greensburg, Penn., 203
Groton, Conn., 170
Guadalupe Hidalgo, Treaty of,
    69
Gulf Intracoastal Waterway, 65
Gulf of Mexico, 64, 90, 115

Hamilton, Alexander, 110
Hardaway, Samuel G., 92
Hardeman, W. P., 138
Hardeman County, Tex., 168
Harpers Ferry, Va., 143, 147
Harriet Lane, USS, 117, 119, 120
Harris County, Tex., 130
Harrisburg, Tex., 83, 130
Harrison, William Henry, 183
Hartford, Conn., 20
Hartford, USS, 97
Harvard University, 173
Hawaii, 172
Hays, Jack, 186, 188
Hays, John Coffee, 18–19, 22
Henry, O., 71–76, 72, 73, 74, 169
Hermitage, the, 183
High Flyer, 48
Hill City Quartette, 73
Hollister, Brother Alonzo, 32
Holly, Buddy, 35–36
Honduras, 75
Honky Tonk Heroes, 38
Horseshoe Bend, Ala., 80
Houston, Sam, 16, 17, 23, 31, 58,
    78–84, 78, 82, 84, 90, 106,
    112–13, 116, 122, 126, 129–33,
    134, 141, 156–57, 159, 160, 163,
    179, 183, 186
Houston Chronicle, 122
Houston Daily Post, 75

Huntsville, Tex., 123
Hurricane Carla, 124

Iliad, 79
Indian Territory, 191
Indianola, Tex., 145
International Business Machines
    Company, 203
International Olympic
    Committee, 26–27
Iran, 203–4
Iturbide, Augustin, 177
Ivins, Molly, 47

Jackson, Andrew, 21, 24, 66, 80,
    81, 156, 182–84
Jackson County, N.C., 194
Jakeway, Bill, 64
Jalapa, Mexico, 177
Jamaica, 179
Jameson, Betty, 25
Jefferson, Thomas, 11
Jennings, Waylon, 35–39, **37**
Jennings, Mrs. Waylon (Jessie
    Coulter), 25
Johnson, Lady Bird, 52–57, 52,
    55, 124–25, **126**
Johnson, Lyndon B., 54–57, **56**
Johnson, R. W., 144
Johnston, Albert Sydney, 143,
    157–58
Jordan, Barbara, 110–14, **112**
Juarez, Benito, 181

Kane, Elisha, **31**
Kansas, 134, 197
Kansas Medical Association, 192
Karankawa Bay, Tex., 82
Karankawas, 58
Karnack, Tex., 53
Karnes, Henry W., 158
Kellam, Jesse, 54–55
Kellogg, Elizabeth, 163
Kennedy, John F., 124

Kerrville high school, 174
KFKB radio station, 192
KHOU television station, 123
Kickapoos, 157
Kimmel, Husband H., 170
King, Amon B., 92
Kiowa-Apaches, 162, 165
Kleburg, Richard, 54
KLLL radio station, 36
Knoxville, Ga., 85
Konopacka, Halina, 27
Kristofferson, Kris, 38
KSAM radio station, 123
KSEL radio station, 36
KTBC television station, 54–57
KTRH radio station, 123

Lafitte, Jean, 58, **59**
Lakeview, Tex., 42
Lamar, Mirabeau B., 15, 130,
    156–61, **158**
Lamar, T. J., 11
Lang, Willis L., 137
LaSalle County, Tex., 72
Law, Richard L., 119
Lea, A. M., 119
Lee, Henry "Light Horse Harry,"
    142
Lee, Mary, **145**
Lee, Robert E., 98, 140, 141–48,
    144, 169
Letcher, John, 147
Lewis, William B., 182
Lexington, Ky., 14
Lincoln, Abraham, 97, 98, 112,
    146
Little Rock, Ark., 13
Littlefield, Tex., 36–37
Lockhart, Matilda, 158
London, 20, 29, 124
Longstreet, James, 169
Los Angeles, Calif., 26, 28
Louisiana Purchase, 11, 69, 82
Lubbock, Tex., 36

Lynn, Loretta, 37

Mackenzie, Ranald, 166–67
Macon, Ga., 86
Macon Telegraph, 87
Macon Volunteers, 85, 87, 89
Magruder, John B., 97, 115–21, **117**, 150
Marks, Leonard, 56
Marshall, Tex., 53
Marshall Plan, 46
Martin, James, 118
Mason City, Iowa, 36
Matamoros, Mex., 67, 68, 104, 189
Maumee, USS, 170
Maury, Matthew Fontaine, 59, **61**
Maximilian Joseph, Ferdinand, 180, **181**
McArthur, Douglas, 172
McCombs, M. J., 26
McCulloch, Ben, 141, 145, 185–91, 190, **191**
McCulloch, Henry E., 142
McLean, Don, 36
McLeod, Hugh, 86–87
McNamara, Robert S., 125
McRae, Alexander, 136
meat biscuit, 29–31
Medicaid, 208
Medicare, 208
Medina River, 105
Mexican War, 24, 85, 134, 143, 189
Mexico City, 16, 66, 68–69, 109, 161, 178–79
Midway Island, 172
Milbank, Jeremiah, 33
Milford, Kans., 192, 194, 195
Military Department of Texas, 190
milk, condensed, 32–33
Milledgeville, Ga., 88
Miller, Alsey, 189

Miller, William P., 93
Miller, W. G., 101
Mission la Bahia, Tex., 91–93
Mississippi River, 30, 94, 149, 161, 186
Mississippi Squadron, 119
Missouri, USS, 173
Mobile, Ala., 11, 87, 99
Mobile Bay, 178
Molino del Rey, Mexico, 69
Monroe, La., 118
Monsanto chemical plant, 48
Monterey, Mexico, 68, 189
Montgomery, Ala., 85
Moore, John H., 101, 186
Moorhead, Minn., 35
Morse, Samuel F. B., 22
Mounted Rifles, 136
Muk-war-rah, 158
Muscogees, 157

Nacogdoches, Tex., 82–83
Naduah, 163
Napoleon III, 180
Nashville, Tenn., 36–38, 80
National Association of Broadcasters, 126
National Youth Administration, 54
Naval War College, 170
Navasota River, 162
Nelson, Willie, 38
Neptune, 118–19
Netherlands, the, 157
Neuces River, 66
Nevada, 70, 134
New Guinea, 172
New Mexico, 66, 70, 134, 135–38
New Orleans, La., 11, 14, 75, 91, 145–46, 149–50
New York, N.Y., 23, 32–33, 71, 76
New York Herald, 149
New York Times, 98
New Washington, Tex., 83

Newsweek, 111
Nimitz, Chester Heinrich, **171**
Nimitz, Chester W., 169–74, 171, **173**
Nixon, Richard M., 110, 125, 126, **127**
Noconis, 163
Northwestern University, 173
Notre Dame, 173

Ochiltree, Thomas P., 135
Ohio, USS, 170
Oklahoma, 134
Oklahoma City, 50
Old Dominion, 120
Olummer, James, 163
Olympic Games, 25–27
On Wings of Eagles, 203
Oo-loo-te-ka, 79
Owasco, USS, 117

Pacific Fleet, 170
Palm Sunday, 93
Palmito Ranch, Tex., 97–102
Palo Alto, Mexico, 68
Palo Duro, Tex., 167
Parker, Benjamin, 162
Parker, Cynthia Ann, 163–64, 167–68
Parker, Granny, 162
Parker, John, 162, 163
Parker, Silas, 162
Parker, Quanah, 159, 162–68, **167**
Parker's Fort, Tex., 163
Patton, Robert S., 87
Pea Ridge, Ark., **191**
Pearl Harbor, Hawaii, 170
Pease River, 163
Pecos, 163–64
Pedernales River, 19
Pelican, Peter, 191
pemmican, 31
Penatekas, 187–89
Pennsylvania, 87

Perot, Ross,. 202–6, **204**
Perot Systems Corporation, 204
Peta Nacona, 163–64
Philadelphia, Pa., 70
Phoenix, Ariz., 36
Pierce, Franklin, 198–99
Plum Creek, Tex., 187
Plummer, Rachel, 163
Plunger, 170
Polk, James K., 24, 66–68, 183–84
Porter, Athol, 74–76
Porter, David D., 119
Porter, Margaret, 76
Porter, William Sydney, 71–76
Post Oak Mission, Tex., 168
Potter, R. M., 145
Price, Norman, 94

Quahadis, 163
Quanah, Acme, and Pacific Railroad, 168
Quanah, Tex., 163, 168

Radke, Lina, 27
Ragnet, Henry W., 136
Raguet, Anna, 83
Randall, Barney, 189
Rangers, Texas, 18–24, 49, 75, 120, 163, 185–86, **187**
Rather, Dan, 122–28, **125**
Raven, the, 79
Read House, 145
Reagan, Ronald, 56
Refugio, Tex., 93
Reily, James, 118
Renshaw, William B., 15, 117
Republic of Texas, 82
Resaca de la Palmas, Mexico, 68
Revolution, Texas, 83–84, 90–94, 103–4, 129–34
revolver, Colt's, 18–24, **22**, 138
revolver, "the Patterson," **22**
revolver, "the Peacemaker," 24
Rice, Grantland, 27

Richards, Ann, 40–45, 41, **44**
Richmond University, 173
Richmond, Va., 118, 155
Rio Grande, 18, 66–69, 98, 99, 103, 135, 136, 157, 178, 189
Ritter, Tex, 37
Roberts, O. M., 101
Robinson, Elizabeth, 27
Robinson, W. N., 101
Rockwell, Norman, 203
Rodgers, Jimmie, 36
Rodino, Peter, 110
Rogers, Ginger, 41
Roosevelt, Theodore, 168
Ross, Sul, 163–64
Rusk, Thomas, 89

Sabine, Tex., 150
Sabine Pass, Tex., 149–55, 151, 152, **153**
Sabine River, 149–53, 151, 152, **153**
Sachem, USS, 117, 150, 153, 154
Saint Louis, Mo., 143
Saltillo, Mexico, 15
Salvation Army, 49
Sam Houston State College, 123
San Antonio de Bexar, 13, 86, 90
San Antonio River, 18, 108.
San Antonio, Tex., 19, 54, 135, 141–42, 145, 156, 158, 186, 190, 200 (*see also* San Antonio de Bexar)
San Felipe de Austin, 16–17, 30, 103 (*see also* Austin)
San Jacinto River, 83, 130–31
San Jacinto, Tex., 16, 58, 87, 88, 89, 94, 129–34, 131, **133**, 178, 186
San Marcos River, 187
Santa Anna, Antonio López de, 15–17, 30, 58, 68, 69, 83, 89, 93, 103–8, 129–34, 156, 176, 177–81, **181**, 189

Santa Anna winds, 177
Sante Fe, N.M., 161, 163
Sante Fe Gazette, 138
Scott, Winfield, 67, 68, 70, 143–44, 146
Scurry, William R., 135
secession, 141, 144–45, 190
Second Cavalry, U.S. Army, 142–43, 163
Second Texas Cavalry, 98
Seminoles, 157f
Seward, William H., 180–81
Shakers, 32
Shanghai, 65
Shawnees, 157
Sherman, Sidney, 130
60 Minutes, 127
Sixty-second Massachusetts Infantry, 100, 119
Slaughter, James E., 97, 99, 101
slaves and slavery, 15, 182–83
Smith, Erastus "Deaf," 131
Smith, Henry, 104, 106
Smithwick, Noah, 30, 33
Solomon Islands, 172
South Vietnam, 124
statehood, 182–84
Steamboat Hotel, 169
Stuart, J. E. B. "Jeb," 143
Swartout, Samuel, 97
Syracuse University, 173

Tampico, 97
Taylor, Claudia Alta (*see* Johnson, Lady Bird)
Taylor, Zachary, 66–70, 67, **69**, 189
Teel, T. T., 135
Telegraph and Texas Land Register, the, 30–31
Texarkana, Tex., 202, 205
Texas City, Tex., 46–50, 48, **49**
Texas Girls' State, 42
Texas Land Office, **74**, 159–60

Texas Revolution, 31, 58
Texas Southern University, 112
Texas State Cemetery, 89
Texas State Women's Golf
  Tournament, 28
Thirty-fourth Indiana Infantry,
  99, 101
This Time, 39
Thomas, Lorenzo, 99
Time, 111
Tokyo, 172
Tokyo Bay, 173,
Tonkawas, 163
Too-nicey, 168
Topsanah, 163–64
Trahan, J. Curtis, 49–50
Transylvania University, 14
Travis County, Tex., 43
Travis, William B., 104–8
Tremont Hotel, 59, 62
Troutman, Joanna, 85–89, **86**
Truman, Harry S., 42
Tubb, Ernest, 36
Tulane University, 173
Twiggs, David, 142–46, 190
Twin Sisters (artillery), 130
Tyler, John, 24, 66, 183–86

U.S. Army, 21, 32–33, 138,
  165–67, 190
U.S. Army Corps of Engineers,
  49–50, 64
U.S. Camel Corps, 200–201
U.S. Civil War Center, 39
U.S. Coast Guard, 50
U.S. Information Agency, 56
U.S. Marines, 143, **147**
U.S. Naval Academy, 170, 171,
  202–3
U.S. Navy, 22, 169–73
U.S. Postal Service, 208
U.S. Signal Service, 149
U.S. State Department, 196f
U.S. Weather Bureau, 60–62

U.S. Women's Amateur Golf
  Tournament, 25, 28
U.S. Women's Open (golf), 28
Ugartechea, 90
Uncle Ben, CSS, 151–53
University of California at
  Berkeley, 170, 174
University of Hawaii, 173
University of Kansas City, 194
University of Texas, 112
University of Texas, Austin, 43,
  53
Urrea, Jose, 91, 93, 129
Utah, 70, 134

Valens, Ritchie, 36
Valverde, N.M., 135–38, **137**
Van Buren, Martin, 70, 183
Van Wie, Virginia, 25
Velasco, 87–88
Venezuela, 179
Vera Cruz, 69, 177–78
Victoria, Tex., 187
Virginia, 144
Virginia Point, 118

Waco, Tex., 41, 42
Wadsworth, William A. O., 87
Wagoner, Porter, 37
Waite, C. A., 146
Walker, John, 98
Walker, Samuel H., 23
Wallace, Lew, 98
Wallace, W. A. A. "Bigfoot," 186
War of 1812, 186
Ward, William, 85, 88, 92–93
Ware, Mass., 20
Washington, D.C., 42, 55, 80, 124,
  167–68, 198
Washington, George, 110
Washington, Martha, 143, 145
Washington Naval Yard, 143
Washington-on-the-Brazos, 16,
  129, 159

Washington Post, 111
Watergate, 127
Waterloo, 159
Watie, Stand, 191
Waylon, the Rambin' Man, 39
Wayne, Henry C., 200
Webster, Daniel, 70
Weddington, Sarah, 43
Weitzel, Godfrey, 150
West Gulf Blockading Squadron, 119
West Point, N.Y., 21, 87, 90, 142–43, 166, 169–70, 171
Westfield, USS, 117, **118**
Wheatley, Phyllis, 113
Whitney, Eli, 22
Williams, Hank, Jr. 38

Williams, John J., 101, **102**
Williams University, 173
Wilson, Woodrow, 110
Wilson B. Keene, 48, 49
Wilson, Robert, 157
Wilson's Creek, 191
Winn, J. C., 88
Woll, Adrian, 18
WSM radio station, 38
Wyoming, 70, 134

XER radio station, 192, **196**

Zaharias, Babe (*see* Didrickson, Mildred)
Zaharias, George, 28
Zapotec, 181

Webb Garrison is a veteran writer who lives in Lake Junaluska, North Carolina. Formerly associate dean of Emory University and president of McKendree College, he has written more than forty books, including *A Treasury of Civil War Tales*, *Civil War Curiosities*, *Lincoln's Little War*, and *Atlanta and the War*.